THE AUSTRALIAN
Women's Weekly

more
slow cooking

One recipe 3 ways – in the slow cooker, oven and on the stove top

CONTENTS

1 RECIPE 3 WAYS

With all the appliances available to us these days, we often take for granted that everyone has the latest gadget on hand. But how many of us don't have a slow cooker... or find the stove top is busy boiling potatoes or steaming beans, or that the oven is otherwise engaged baking a cake or pudding for dessert?

With this in mind, we have developed this book so all bases are covered – one recipe has been converted so it can be cooked on the stove top, in the oven, or in a slow cooker. Many of the recipes have small, but significant, differences in the ingredient list or in the method of cooking, so it's important you use the correct instructions for that recipe.

Throughout this book we used two different-sized slow cookers: a 4.5-litre (18-cup) and a 5-litre (20-cup) – all the slow cooker recipes can be cooked in either of these sized cookers. If using any other sized cooker, you will need to increase or decrease the quantity of liquid in the recipe, and possibly the amount of food.

The best type of pot to use when cooking on the stove top is a heavy-based casserole dish or dutch oven. These contain and distribute the heat evenly. The lid must fit the dish tightly to seal in the flavours and moisture.

Slow cooking in the oven is another great 'set and forget' form of cooking. As with slow cooking on the stove top, a heavy-based casserole or dutch oven will ensure that the pot holds and evenly distributes the heat while cooking in the oven. One convenience when cooking on the stove top or in the oven is that you use the same dish to brown the meat that you cook in...so no extra washing up.

These days some slow cooker appliances have an insert that can be used to brown the meat on the stove top before being inserted into the cooker to continue cooking. But, if you haven't got one of these, not to worry, we developed the slow cooker recipes in this book as 'straight in lid on'...no pre-browning necessary.

THE BEST SLOW COOKING CUTS

Long, slow cooking will tenderise even the toughest cut of meat. Tough cuts, such as stewing or braising meats, are usually inexpensive. Be sure to trim off any visible fat and cut the pieces into a uniform size.

The best cuts of meat to use are:
Beef: topside, oyster, blade, round, chuck, skirt and gravy beef.
Veal: osso buco, shanks, shoulder.
Lamb: neck chops, boneless shoulder, shanks, boneless forequarter.

Pork: forequarter chops, neck, belly, shoulder. Chicken: any pieces on the bone, such as thighs, drumsticks, marylands; whole chickens are also fine, too. Other cuts: venison, kangaroo, goat, rabbit, hare, buffalo, etc.

USING DRIED BEANS

If using dried beans, be aware that some need to be cooked before adding to the recipe because of a certain chemical they contain. Kidney-shaped beans of all colours and sizes are related to each other and must be washed, drained and boiled in fresh water until tender before adding to the cooker or pot. Once cooked, they can be safely added to the recipe, just like canned beans. Soya beans and chickpeas are fine to use raw, just rinse well first; there's no need for overnight soaking before cooking them slowly.

FREEZING LEFTOVERS

One great benefit of slow cooking is that you can cook a large amount of food at once. This allows you to feed large groups of people or, alternatively, have leftovers that you can freeze for another time.

If frozen properly, slow-cooked meals will keep for up to 3 months. There is usually a large quantity of liquid, so remove the meat and vegetables to appropriate-sized freezer-friendly containers, pour in enough of the liquid to cover the meat etc, seal the container, and freeze, remembering to label and date the container. Any sauce that is left over can be frozen separately and used as a base for another recipe such as a soup or a sauce.

TAKING OUT THE FAT

When cooking meats over a long period of time they can often produce a lot of fat, which you will need to remove. The best fat removal method is to refrigerate the food; the fat will set on top of the liquid, and then it can simply be lifted off and discarded. If you don't have the time to refrigerate the food before serving, there are a couple of gadgets available in kitchen/cookware shops for removing fat: one is a type of 'brush' that sweeps away the fat; the other is a type of jug that separates the fat from the liquid. One of the easiest ways to remove fat is to soak it up using sheets of absorbent kitchen paper – cheap and effective.

USING YOUR FAVOURITE RECIPES

Most of your favourite soup, stew, tagine and curry recipes are suitable to slow cook, even if you're not used to cooking them this way. You may need to adjust the liquid content to accommodate the long, slow, cooking times, but once you get to know how your chosen method works in the oven, slow cooker, or on the stove top, the possibilities are endless.

BEEF & VEAL

IN THE SLOW COOKER

beer & thyme beef cheeks

PREP + COOK TIME 10½ HOURS **SERVES** 6

16 baby onions (400g)

3 stalks celery (450g), trimmed, chopped coarsely

400g (12½ ounces) baby carrots, trimmed

4 sprigs fresh thyme

1½ cups (375ml) beer

1 cup (250ml) beef stock

¼ cup (70g) tomato paste

2 tablespoons worcestershire sauce

1 tablespoon brown sugar

1 tablespoon wholegrain mustard

2kg (4 pounds) trimmed beef cheeks

150g (4½ ounces) green beans, trimmed

1 Peel onions, leaving root end intact. Combine onions with celery, carrots, thyme, beer, stock, tomato paste, sauce, sugar and mustard in a 5-litre (20-cup) slow cooker. Add beef; turn to coat in mixture. Cook, covered, on low, for 9½ hours.

2 Discard thyme. Add beans to cooker; cook, covered, on low, for 30 minutes. Season to taste. Serve beef sprinkled with extra fresh thyme.

tip You will need 1 bunch of baby carrots. They may also be sold as 'dutch' carrots.

serving suggestion Creamy mashed potato or cheesy polenta.

freezing: all versions are suitable to freeze.

IN THE OVEN

beer & thyme beef cheeks

PREP + COOK TIME 4 HOURS SERVES 6

¼ cup (35g) plain (all-purpose) flour

2kg (4 pounds) trimmed beef cheeks

2 tablespoons olive oil

16 baby onions (400g)

1½ cups (375ml) beer

2½ cups (625ml) beef stock

3 stalks celery (450g), trimmed, chopped coarsely

400g (12½ ounces) baby carrots, trimmed

4 sprigs fresh thyme

¼ cup (70g) tomato paste

2 tablespoons worcestershire sauce

1 tablespoon brown sugar

1 tablespoon wholegrain mustard

150g (4½ ounces) green beans, trimmed

1 Preheat oven to 180°C/350°F.
2 Season flour in a large bowl; dust beef in flour, shake off excess. Heat half the oil in a large flameproof casserole dish over high heat on the stove top; cook beef, in batches, until browned. Remove from dish.
3 Meanwhile, peel onions, leaving root end intact.
4 Heat remaining oil in dish; cook onions, stirring, until browned. Add beer; bring to the boil, stirring. Return beef to dish with stock, celery, carrots, thyme, tomato paste, sauce, sugar and mustard; bring to the boil. Cover dish, transfer to oven.
5 Cook, covered, for 2½ hours. Uncover; cook, in oven, a further 30 minutes or until beef is tender.
6 Discard thyme. Add beans to dish; cook, in oven, uncovered, for 5 minutes or until beans are tender. Season; serve beef sprinkled with extra fresh thyme.

ON THE STOVE TOP

beer & thyme beef cheeks

PREP + COOK TIME 4 HOURS SERVES 6

¼ cup (35g) plain (all-purpose) flour

2kg (4 pounds) trimmed beef cheeks

2 tablespoons olive oil

16 baby onions (400g)

1½ cups (375ml) beer

2½ cups (625ml) beef stock

3 stalks celery (450g), trimmed, chopped coarsely

400g (12½ ounces) baby carrots, trimmed

4 sprigs fresh thyme

¼ cup (70g) tomato paste

2 tablespoons worcestershire sauce

1 tablespoon brown sugar

1 tablespoon wholegrain mustard

150g (4½ ounces) green beans, trimmed

1 Season flour in a large bowl; dust beef in flour, shake off excess. Heat half the oil in a large saucepan over high heat; cook beef, in batches, until browned. Remove from pan.
2 Meanwhile, peel onions, leaving root end intact.
3 Heat remaining oil in pan; cook onions, stirring, until browned. Add beer; bring to the boil, stirring. Return beef to pan with stock, celery, carrots, thyme, tomato paste, sauce, sugar and mustard; bring to the boil. Reduce heat; simmer, covered, for 2½ hours. Uncover; simmer a further 30 minutes or until beef is tender.
4 Discard thyme. Add beans to pan; simmer, uncovered, for 5 minutes or until beans are tender. Season; serve beef sprinkled with extra fresh thyme.

hoisin sauce

garlic

orange

brown sugar

buk choy

star anise

long red chilli

oxtail

black pepper

dry sherry

beef stock

green onion (scallion)

10

hoisin & star anise oxtail

nutritional count per serving
- ▶ 59.8g total fat
- ▶ 22.5g saturated fat
- ▶ 3850kJ (921 cal)
- ▶ 40.5g carbohydrate
- ▶ 50.3g protein
- ▶ 5.1g fibre

IN THE SLOW COOKER

hoisin & star anise oxtail

PREP + COOK TIME 9½ HOURS SERVES 4

2kg (4 pounds) oxtails, cut into 5cm (2-inch) pieces

⅔ cup (160ml) hoisin sauce

1 cup (250ml) beef stock

¼ cup (60ml) dry sherry

1 tablespoon finely grated orange rind

⅓ cup (80ml) orange juice

3 cloves garlic, crushed

2 tablespoons brown sugar

½ teaspoon cracked black pepper

2 star anise

500g (1 pound) buk choy, trimmed, quartered lengthways

1 fresh long red chilli, sliced thinly

3 green onions (scallions), sliced thinly

1 Trim excess fat from oxtail. Pack oxtail tightly, in a single layer, in the base of a 5-litre (20-cup) slow cooker. Whisk sauce, stock, sherry, rind, juice, garlic, sugar and pepper in a medium jug until combined; add star anise. Pour mixture over oxtail in cooker. Cook, covered, on low, for 8 hours.

2 Discard star anise. Remove oxtail; cover to keep warm. Skim fat from surface of liquid in cooker. Add buk choy to cooker; cook, uncovered, on high, for 5 minutes or until wilted.

3 Return oxtail to cooker; cook, uncovered, on high, until oxtail is heated through. Season to taste. Serve oxtail with buk choy and cooking liquid. Sprinkle with chilli and green onions.

tip To thicken the liquid, uncover the cooker for the last hour of cooking in step 1.
serving suggestion Steamed rice
freezing: all versions are suitable to freeze.

IN THE OVEN

hoisin & star anise oxtail

PREP + COOK TIME 4 HOURS **SERVES** 4

2kg (4 pounds) oxtails, cut into 5cm (2-inch) pieces

⅔ cup (160ml) hoisin sauce

1 cup (250ml) beef stock

¼ cup (60ml) dry sherry

1 tablespoon finely grated orange rind

⅓ cup (80ml) orange juice

3 cloves garlic, crushed

2 tablespoons brown sugar

½ teaspoon cracked black pepper

2 star anise

500g (1 pound) buk choy, trimmed, quartered lengthways

1 fresh long red chilli, sliced thinly

3 green onions (scallions), sliced thinly

1 Preheat oven to 180°C/350°F.
2 Trim excess fat from oxtail. Pack oxtail tightly, in a single layer, in the base of a large flameproof casserole dish. Whisk sauce, stock, sherry, rind, juice, garlic, sugar and pepper in a medium jug until combined; add star anise. Pour mixture over oxtail. Bring to the boil. Cover dish, transfer to oven; cook, covered, for 3½ hours or until oxtail is tender.
3 Discard star anise. Remove oxtail; cover to keep warm. Skim fat from surface of liquid. Add buk choy to dish; simmer, uncovered, on stove top for 5 minutes or until wilted. Return oxtail to dish; cook, uncovered, over high heat, until oxtail is heated through, season.
4 Serve oxtail with buk choy and cooking liquid. Sprinkle with chilli and green onions.

ON THE STOVE TOP

hoisin & star anise oxtail

PREP + COOK TIME 3½ HOURS **SERVES** 4

2kg (4 pounds) oxtails, cut into 5cm (2-inch) pieces

⅔ cup (160ml) hoisin sauce

1 cup (250ml) beef stock

¼ cup (60ml) dry sherry

1 tablespoon finely grated orange rind

⅓ cup (80ml) orange juice

3 cloves garlic, crushed

2 tablespoons brown sugar

½ teaspoon cracked black pepper

2 star anise

500g (1 pound) buk choy, trimmed, quartered lengthways

1 fresh long red chilli, sliced thinly

3 green onions (scallions), sliced thinly

1 Trim excess fat from oxtail. Pack oxtail tightly, in a single layer, in the base of a large heavy-based saucepan. Whisk sauce, stock, sherry, rind, juice, garlic, sugar and pepper in a medium jug until combined. Add star anise; pour mixture over oxtail.
2 Bring to the boil. Reduce heat; simmer, covered, for 3 hours or until oxtail is tender.
3 Discard star anise. Remove oxtail; cover to keep warm. Skim fat from surface of liquid. Add buk choy to pan; simmer, uncovered, for 5 minutes or until wilted.
4 Return oxtail to pan; simmer, uncovered, until oxtail is heated through; season.
5 Serve oxtail with buk choy and cooking liquid. Sprinkle with chilli and green onions.

IN THE SLOW COOKER

vietnamese beef brisket

PREP + COOK TIME 9¾ HOURS SERVES 4

1.5kg (3 pounds) beef brisket, trimmed, cut into 5cm (2-inch) pieces

1 large brown onion (200g), sliced thinly

3 cloves garlic, crushed

4 teaspoons finely grated fresh ginger

1 fresh long red chilli, sliced thinly

2 x 10cm (4-inch) stalks fresh lemon grass (40g), halved lengthways

2 fresh kaffir lime leaves, bruised

2 star anise

1 cinnamon stick

2 tablespoons grated palm sugar

¼ cup (60ml) fish sauce

¼ cup (60ml) dark soy sauce

3 cups (750ml) beef stock

1 large red capsicum (bell pepper) (350g), chopped coarsely

125g (4 ounces) baby corn, halved

150g (4½ ounces) snake beans, chopped coarsely

⅓ cup coarsely chopped roasted unsalted peanuts

⅓ cup loosely packed fresh coriander leaves (cilantro)

1 lime, cut into wedges, to serve

1 Combine beef, onion, garlic, ginger, chilli, lemon grass, kaffir lime leaves, star anise, cinnamon, sugar, sauces, stock, capsicum and corn in a 5-litre (20-cup) slow cooker. Cook, covered, on low, for 9 hours.

2 Add beans to cooker; cook, covered, a further 30 minutes.

3 Discard lemon grass, kaffir lime leaves, star anise and cinnamon; season to taste. To serve, sprinkle beef with nuts and coriander; accompany with lime wedges.

freezing: all versions are suitable to freeze.

nutritional count per serving
▶ 36.9g total fat
▶ 10.6g saturated fat
▶ 3319kJ (794 cal)
▶ 24.8g carbohydrate
▶ 88g protein
▶ 6.9g fibre

vietnamese beef brisket

PREP + COOK TIME 2½ HOURS SERVES 4

2 tablespoons vegetable or peanut oil

1.5kg (3 pounds) beef brisket, trimmed, cut into 5cm (2-inch) pieces

1 large brown onion (200g), sliced thinly

3 cloves garlic, crushed

4 teaspoons finely grated fresh ginger

1 fresh long red chilli, sliced thinly

2 x 10cm (4-inch) stalks fresh lemon grass (40g), halved lengthways

2 fresh kaffir lime leaves, bruised

2 star anise

1 cinnamon stick

2 tablespoons grated palm sugar

¼ cup (60ml) fish sauce

¼ cup (60ml) dark soy sauce

3 cups (750ml) beef stock

1 large red capsicum (bell pepper) (350g), chopped coarsely

125g (4 ounces) baby corn, halved

150g (4½ ounces) snake beans, chopped coarsely

⅓ cup coarsely chopped roasted unsalted peanuts

⅓ cup loosely packed fresh coriander leaves (cilantro)

1 lime, cut into wedges, to serve

1 Preheat oven to 180°C/350°F.

2 Heat half the oil in a large flameproof casserole dish, over high heat, on the stove top; cook beef, in batches, until browned. Remove from dish.

3 Heat remaining oil in dish over low heat; cook onion, garlic, ginger and chilli, stirring, until onion softens. Return beef to dish with lemon grass, kaffir lime leaves, star anise, cinnamon, sugar, sauces and stock; bring to the boil.

4 Cover dish, transfer to oven; cook, covered, for 2 hours or until beef is tender.

5 Add capsicum, corn and beans to dish, return to oven; cook, uncovered, for 15 minutes or until vegetables are tender.

6 Discard lemon grass, kaffir lime leaves, star anise and cinnamon. Season to taste. Serve beef sprinkled with nuts and coriander; accompany with lime wedges.

ON THE STOVE TOP

vietnamese beef brisket

PREP + COOK TIME 2½ HOURS SERVES 4

2 tablespoons vegetable or peanut oil

1.5kg (3 pounds) beef brisket, trimmed, cut into 5cm (2-inch) pieces

1 large brown onion (200g), sliced thinly

3 cloves garlic, crushed

4 teaspoons finely grated fresh ginger

1 fresh long red chilli, sliced thinly

2 x 10cm (4-inch) stalks fresh lemon grass (40g), halved lengthways

2 fresh kaffir lime leaves, bruised

2 star anise

1 cinnamon stick

2 tablespoons grated palm sugar

¼ cup (60ml) fish sauce

¼ cup (60ml) dark soy sauce

3 cups (750ml) beef stock

1 large red capsicum (bell pepper) (350g), chopped coarsely

125g (4 ounces) baby corn, halved

150g (4½ ounces) snake beans, chopped coarsely

⅓ cup coarsely chopped roasted unsalted peanuts

⅓ cup loosely packed fresh coriander leaves (cilantro)

1 lime, cut into wedges, to serve

1 Heat half the oil in a large saucepan over high heat; cook beef, in batches, until browned. Remove from pan.

2 Heat remaining oil in pan over low heat; cook onion, garlic, ginger and chilli, stirring, until onion softens. Return beef to pan with lemon grass, kaffir lime leaves, star anise, cinnamon, sugar, sauces and stock; bring to the boil. Reduce heat; simmer, covered, for 2 hours or until beef is tender.

3 Add capsicum, corn and beans to pan; simmer, uncovered, for 15 minutes or until tender.

4 Discard lemon grass, kaffir lime leaves, star anise and cinnamon. Season to taste. Serve beef sprinkled with nuts and coriander; accompany with lime wedges.

IN THE SLOW COOKER

spanish oxtail and chickpea soup

PREP + COOK TIME 8¾ HOURS SERVES 6

1.5kg (3 pounds) oxtails, cut into 5cm (2-inch) pieces

400g (12½ ounces) canned chickpeas (garbanzo beans), rinsed, drained

400g (12½ ounces) canned diced tomatoes

2 small leeks (400g), sliced thinly

2 medium carrots (240g), halved, sliced thickly

½ cup (100g) thinly sliced roasted red capsicum (bell pepper)

3 cloves garlic, crushed

2 dried bay leaves

2 teaspoons smoked paprika

1 teaspoon dried chilli flakes

½ cup (125ml) dry sherry

1 litre (4 cups) water

2 cups (500ml) beef stock

250g (8 ounces) packaged microwave white long-grain rice

1 cured chorizo sausage (130g), sliced thinly

⅓ cup loosely packed fresh flat-leaf parsley leaves

1 lemon, cut into wedges, to serve

1 Trim excess fat from oxtail. Combine oxtail, chickpeas, tomatoes, leek, carrot, capsicum, garlic, bay leaves, paprika, chilli flakes, sherry, the water and stock in a 5-litre (20-cup) slow cooker. Cook, covered, on low, for 8 hours.

2 Heat rice according to directions on packet.

3 Meanwhile, discard bay leaves from cooker. Skim fat from surface. Add rice to cooker; cook, uncovered, on high, for 5 minutes or until mixture is thickened slightly. Season to taste.

4 Cook chorizo in a heated small frying pan until browned and crisp; drain on absorbent paper. Divide oxtail into serving bowls; ladle hot soup into bowls. Serve soup topped with chorizo and parsley; accompany with lemon wedges, and warm crusty bread, if you like.

tips You'll want to use a spoon and fork to eat this soup, as it's a rustic, hearty meal on its own; If the soup is a little thick you could add a little more water or stock.
freezing: all versions are suitable to freeze.

nutritional count per serving
▶ 34.8g total fat
▶ 12.7g saturated fat
▶ 2500kJ (598 cal)
▶ 28.7g carbohydrate
▶ 33.9g protein
▶ 4.7g fibre

spanish oxtail and chickpea soup

PREP + COOK TIME 3¾ HOURS SERVES 6

1.5kg (3 pounds) oxtails, cut into 5cm (2-inch) pieces

400g (12½ ounces) canned chickpeas (garbanzo beans), rinsed, drained

400g (12½ ounces) canned diced tomatoes

2 small leeks (400g), sliced thinly

2 medium carrots (240g), halved, sliced thickly

½ cup (100g) thinly sliced roasted red capsicum (bell pepper)

3 cloves garlic, crushed

2 dried bay leaves

2 teaspoons smoked paprika

1 teaspoon dried chilli flakes

½ cup (125ml) dry sherry

1 litre (4 cups) water

2 cups (500ml) beef stock

250g (8 ounces) packaged microwave white long-grain rice

1 cured chorizo sausage (130g), sliced thinly

⅓ cup loosely packed fresh flat-leaf parsley leaves

1 lemon, cut into wedges, to serve

1 Preheat oven to 180°C/350°F.

2 Trim excess fat from oxtail. Combine oxtail, chickpeas, tomatoes, leek, carrot, capsicum, garlic, bay leaves, paprika, chilli flakes, sherry, the water and stock in a large flameproof casserole dish; bring to the boil on the stove top.

3 Cover dish, transfer to oven; cook, covered, for 3 hours or until oxtail is tender.

4 Heat rice according to directions on packet.

5 Meanwhile, discard bay leaves from dish. Skim fat from surface. Add rice to dish; simmer, uncovered, on stove top, for 5 minutes or until thickened slightly. Season to taste.

6 Cook chorizo in a heated small frying pan until browned and crisp; drain on absorbent paper. Divide oxtail into serving bowls; ladle hot soup into bowls. Serve soup topped with chorizo and parsley; accompany with lemon wedges, and warm crusty bread, if you like.

ON THE STOVE TOP

spanish oxtail and chickpea soup

PREP + COOK TIME 3¾ HOURS SERVES 6

1.5kg (3 pounds) oxtails, cut into 5cm (2-inch) pieces

400g (12½ ounces) canned chickpeas (garbanzo beans), rinsed, drained

400g (12½ ounces) canned diced tomatoes

2 small leeks (400g), sliced thinly

2 medium carrots (240g), halved, sliced thickly

½ cup (100g) thinly sliced roasted red capsicum (bell pepper)

3 cloves garlic, crushed

2 dried bay leaves

2 teaspoons smoked paprika

1 teaspoon dried chilli flakes

½ cup (125ml) dry sherry

1 litre (4 cups) water

2 cups (500ml) beef stock

250g (8 ounces) packaged microwave white long-grain rice

1 cured chorizo sausage (130g), sliced thinly

⅓ cup loosely packed fresh flat-leaf parsley leaves

1 lemon, cut into wedges, to serve

1 Trim excess fat from oxtail. Combine oxtail, chickpeas, tomatoes, leek, carrot, capsicum, garlic, bay leaves, paprika, chilli flakes, sherry, the water and stock in a large saucepan; bring to the boil. Reduce heat; simmer, covered, for 3 hours or until oxtail is tender.

2 Heat rice according to directions on packet.

3 Meanwhile, discard bay leaves from pan. Skim fat from surface. Add rice to pan; simmer, uncovered, for 5 minutes or until thickened slightly, season.

4 Cook chorizo in a heated small frying pan until browned and crisp; drain on absorbent paper. Divide oxtail into serving bowls; ladle hot soup into bowls. Serve soup topped with chorizo and parsley; accompany with lemon wedges, and warm crusty bread, if you like.

IN THE SLOW COOKER

beef and vegetable soup

PREP + COOK TIME 9¾ HOURS SERVES 4

1kg (2 pounds) gravy beef, trimmed, cut into 2.5cm (1-inch) pieces

1 clove garlic, crushed

1 medium brown onion (150g), cut into 1cm (½-inch) pieces

2 stalks celery (300g), trimmed, cut into 1cm (½-inch) pieces

2 medium carrots (240g), cut into 1cm (½-inch) pieces

2 medium potatoes (400g), cut into 1cm (½-inch) pieces

400g (12½ ounces) canned diced tomatoes

1 litre (4 cups) water

2 cups (500ml) beef stock

2 dried bay leaves

1 cup (120g) frozen peas

⅓ cup coarsely chopped fresh flat-leaf parsley

1 Combine beef, garlic, onion, celery, carrot, potato, tomatoes, the water, stock and bay leaves in a 5-litre (20-cup) slow cooker. Cook, covered, on low, for 9 hours.

2 Add peas to cooker; cook, covered, for a further 30 minutes.

3 Discard bay leaves. Season to taste. Serve soup sprinkled with parsley; accompany with thick slices of crusty bread, if you like.

freezing: all versions are suitable to freeze.

nutritional count per serving
- ▶ 14.5g total fat
- ▶ 5.4g saturated fat
- ▶ 1940kJ (464 cal)
- ▶ 20.9g carbohydrate
- ▶ 57.4g protein
- ▶ 8.9g fibre

IN THE OVEN

beef and vegetable soup

PREP + COOK TIME 3 HOURS SERVES 4

1kg (2 pounds) gravy beef, trimmed, cut into 2.5cm (1-inch) pieces

1 clove garlic, crushed

1 medium brown onion (150g), cut into 1cm (½-inch) pieces

2 stalks celery (300g), trimmed, cut into 1cm (½-inch) pieces

2 medium carrots (240g), cut into 1cm (½-inch) pieces

2 medium potatoes (400g), cut into 1cm (½-inch) pieces

400g (12½ ounces) canned diced tomatoes

1 litre (4 cups) water

2 cups (500ml) beef stock

2 dried bay leaves

1 cup (120g) frozen peas

⅓ cup coarsely chopped fresh flat-leaf parsley

1 Preheat oven to 180°C/350°F.
2 Combine beef, garlic, onion, celery, carrot, potato, tomatoes, the water, stock and bay leaves in a large flameproof casserole dish; bring to the boil on the stove top.
3 Cover dish, transfer to oven; cook, covered, for 2½ hours or until beef is tender. Add peas to dish; stand, covered, for 5 minutes or until peas are tender.
4 Discard bay leaves. Season to taste. Serve soup sprinkled with parsley; accompany with thick slices of crusty bread, if you like.

ON THE STOVE TOP

beef and vegetable soup

PREP + COOK TIME 3 HOURS SERVES 4

1kg (2 pounds) gravy beef, trimmed, cut into 2.5cm (1-inch) pieces

1 clove garlic, crushed

1 medium brown onion (150g), cut into 1cm (½-inch) pieces

2 stalks celery (300g), trimmed, cut into 1cm (½-inch) pieces

2 medium carrots (240g), cut into 1cm (½-inch) pieces

2 medium potatoes (400g), cut into 1cm (½-inch) pieces

400g (12½ ounces) canned diced tomatoes

1 litre (4 cups) water

2 cups (500ml) beef stock

2 dried bay leaves

1 cup (120g) frozen peas

⅓ cup coarsely chopped fresh flat-leaf parsley

1 Combine beef, garlic, onion, celery, carrot, potato, tomatoes, the water, stock and bay leaves in a large saucepan; bring to the boil. Reduce heat; simmer, covered, for 2½ hours or until beef is tender.
2 Add peas to pan; simmer, uncovered, for about 5 minutes or until peas are tender.
3 Discard bay leaves. Season to taste. Serve soup sprinkled with parsley; accompany with thick slices of crusty bread, if you like.

thyme sprigs

bay leaves

beef stock

bacon slices

flat-leaf parsley

tomato paste

beef short ribs

swiss brown & button mushrooms

shallots

garlic

dry red wine

26

beef rib bourguignon

nutritional count per serving

▶ 47.8g total fat
▶ 16.2g saturated fat
▶ 3106kJ (743 cal)
▶ 6g carbohydrate
▶ 60.9g protein
▶ 4.3g fibre

beef rib bourguignon

PREP + COOK TIME 2½ HOURS SERVES 4

2 tablespoons olive oil

1.2kg (2½ pounds) beef short ribs

12 shallots (300g)

4 rindless bacon slices (260g), cut into 5cm (2-inch) lengths

200g (6½ ounces) button mushrooms

200g (6½ ounces) swiss brown mushrooms

3 cloves garlic, sliced thinly

2 fresh thyme sprigs

2 fresh bay leaves

1½ cups (375ml) dry red wine

2 cups (500ml) beef stock

2 tablespoons tomato paste

½ cup finely chopped fresh flat-leaf parsley

1 Preheat oven to 180°C/350°F. Heat half the oil in a large flameproof casserole dish over high heat on the stove top; cook beef until browned. Remove from dish.

2 Heat remaining oil in dish; cook shallots, bacon and mushrooms, stirring, until browned lightly. Add garlic, thyme and bay leaves to dish; cook, stirring, for 1 minute or until fragrant.

3 Add wine to dish; bring to the boil. Reduce heat; simmer, uncovered, for 2 minutes or until wine is reduced by half. Return beef to dish with stock and paste; bring to the boil.

4 Cover dish, transfer to oven; cook for 1½ hours. Uncover; return to oven; cook a further 30 minutes or until beef is tender and sauce has thickened.

5 Discard thyme and bay leaves. Stir in half the parsley; season to taste. Serve beef sprinkled with remaining parsley.

tip Cut the shallots in half if they are large.
serving suggestion Mashed potatoes or steamed baby new potatoes, and crusty bread.
freezing: all versions are unsuitable to freeze.

IN THE SLOW COOKER

beef rib bourguignon

PREP + COOK TIME 8½ HOURS SERVES 4

12 shallots (300g)

200g (6½ ounces) button mushrooms

200g (6½ ounces) swiss brown mushrooms

4 rindless bacon slices (260g), cut into 5cm (2-inch) lengths

3 cloves garlic, sliced thinly

2 fresh thyme sprigs

2 fresh bay leaves

1½ cups (375ml) dry red wine

3 cups (750ml) beef stock

2 tablespoons tomato paste

1.2kg (2½ pounds) beef short ribs

½ cup finely chopped fresh flat-leaf parsley

1 Place shallots, mushrooms, bacon, garlic, thyme, bay leaves, wine, stock, paste and beef in a 4.5-litre (18-cup) slow cooker. Cook, covered, on low, for 8 hours. Season to taste.
2 Discard thyme and bay leaves. Stir in half the parsley; season to taste. Serve topped with the remaining parsley.

ON THE STOVE TOP

beef rib bourguignon

PREP + COOK TIME 2½ HOURS SERVES 4

2 tablespoons olive oil

1.2kg (2½ pounds) beef short ribs

12 shallots (300g)

4 rindless bacon slices (260g), cut into 5cm (2-inch) lengths

3 cloves garlic, sliced thinly

2 fresh thyme sprigs

2 fresh bay leaves

1½ cups (375ml) dry red wine

2 cups (500ml) beef stock

2 tablespoons tomato paste

200g (6½ ounces) swiss brown mushrooms

200g (6½ ounces) button mushrooms

½ cup finely chopped fresh flat-leaf parsley

1 Heat half the oil in a large saucepan over high heat; cook beef until browned. Remove from pan.
2 Heat remaining oil in pan; cook shallots and bacon, stirring, until browned lightly. Add garlic, thyme and bay leaves; cook, stirring, for 1 minute or until fragrant.
3 Add wine to pan; bring to the boil. Reduce heat; simmer, uncovered, for 2 minutes or until liquid is reduced by half. Return beef to pan with stock and paste; bring to the boil. Reduce heat; simmer, covered, for 1½ hours. Add mushrooms; simmer, uncovered, a further 30 minutes or until beef is tender and sauce has thickened.
4 Discard thyme and bay leaves. Stir in half the parsley; season to taste. Sprinkle with remaining parsley to serve.

IN THE OVEN

coconut curried beef

PREP + COOK TIME 2½ HOURS SERVES 4

2 tablespoons olive oil

1kg (2 pounds) diced beef

4 teaspoons finely grated fresh ginger

3 cloves garlic, crushed

2 medium brown onions (300g), cut into thin wedges

2 tablespoons thai yellow curry paste

2 cups (500ml) beef stock

400ml (12½ ounces) canned coconut milk

2 fresh kaffir lime leaves

8 fresh curry leaves

2 tablespoons fish sauce

2 tablespoons grated palm sugar

150g (4½ ounces) snow peas

2 tablespoons finely chopped peanuts, toasted

¼ cup firmly packed fresh thai basil leaves

1 fresh long red chilli, sliced thinly

1 Preheat oven to 180°C/350°F. Heat half the oil in a large flameproof casserole dish over high heat on the stove top; cook beef, in batches, until browned. Remove from dish.

2 Heat remaining oil in dish; cook ginger, garlic and onion, stirring, until softened. Add paste; cook, stirring, for 1 minute or until fragrant.

3 Return beef to dish with stock, coconut milk, kaffir lime leaves and curry leaves; bring to the boil. Cover dish, transfer to oven; cook for 1½ hours. Uncover, return to oven; cook a further 15 minutes or until beef is tender and sauce has thickened.

4 Discard lime leaves. Stir in sauce, sugar and snow peas. Stand, covered, for 5 minutes or until snow peas are tender. Season to taste. Serve beef topped with peanuts, basil and chilli.

serving suggestion **Serve on fresh rice noodles or steamed jasmine rice, accompanied with lime wedges.**
freezing: **all versions are unsuitable to freeze.**

nutritional count per serving
- ▶ 46.5g total fat
- ▶ 22.5g saturated fat
- ▶ 3043kJ (728 cal)
- ▶ 17.3g carbohydrate
- ▶ 59.2g protein
- ▶ 5g fibre

IN THE SLOW COOKER

coconut curried beef

PREP + COOK TIME 10¾ HOURS **SERVES** 4

1kg (2 pounds) diced beef

2 tablespoons thai yellow curry paste

1⅔ cups (410ml) coconut milk

2 cups (500ml) beef stock

4 teaspoons finely grated fresh ginger

3 cloves garlic, crushed

2 medium brown onions (300g), cut into thin wedges

2 fresh kaffir lime leaves

8 fresh curry leaves

2 tablespoons fish sauce

2 tablespoons grated palm sugar

150g (4½ ounces) snow peas

2 tablespoons finely chopped peanuts, toasted

¼ cup firmly packed fresh thai basil leaves

1 fresh long red chilli, sliced thinly

1 Place beef, paste and coconut milk in a 4.5-litre (18-cup) slow cooker; stir until paste dissolves.
2 Add stock, ginger, garlic, onion, kaffir lime leaves, curry leaves, sauce and sugar to cooker. Cook, covered, on high, for 2 hours. Reduce to low; cook for a further 8 hours. Season to taste.
3 Discard lime leaves. Stir in snow peas; cook, covered, on low, for 10 minutes or until peas are tender. Season to taste. Serve beef topped with peanuts, basil and chilli.

ON THE STOVE TOP

coconut curried beef

PREP + COOK TIME 2¾ HOURS **SERVES** 4

2 tablespoons olive oil

1kg (2 pounds) diced beef

4 teaspoons finely grated fresh ginger

3 cloves garlic, crushed

2 medium brown onions (300g), cut into thin wedges

2 tablespoons thai yellow curry paste

2 cups (500ml) beef stock

1⅔ cups (410ml) coconut milk

2 fresh kaffir lime leaves

8 fresh curry leaves

2 tablespoons fish sauce

2 tablespoons grated palm sugar

150g (4½ ounces) snow peas

2 tablespoons finely chopped peanuts, toasted

¼ cup firmly packed fresh thai basil leaves

1 fresh long red chilli, sliced thinly

1 Heat half the oil in a large saucepan over high heat; cook beef, in batches until browned. Remove from pan. Heat remaining oil in pan; cook ginger, garlic and onion, stirring, until softened. Add paste; cook, stirring, for 1 minute or until fragrant.
2 Return beef to pan with stock, coconut milk, kaffir lime leaves and curry leaves; bring to the boil. Reduce heat; simmer, covered, for 1½ hours. Uncover; simmer for 20 minutes or until beef is tender and sauce has thickened.
3 Discard lime leaves. Add sauce, sugar and snow peas; cook, uncovered, for 5 minutes or until peas are tender. Season to taste. Serve beef topped with peanuts, basil and chilli.

IN THE SLOW COOKER

mexican beef chilli mole

PREP + COOK TIME 8¾ HOURS SERVES 4

1kg (2 pounds) beef chuck steak, cut into
3cm (1¼-inch) cubes

2 cups (500ml) beef stock

2 cups (500ml) water

3 chipotle peppers in adobo sauce, chopped finely

4 rindless bacon slices (260g), chopped coarsely

1 medium brown onion (150g), chopped finely

4 cloves garlic, crushed

2 tablespoons tomato paste

439g (14 ounces) canned black beans,
rinsed, drained

410g (13 ounces) tomato puree

2 teaspoons each ground cumin, coriander and
sweet smoked paprika

¼ teaspoon chilli powder

½ teaspoon ground cinnamon

2 tablespoons finely grated mexican chocolate

⅔ cup (80g) grated manchego cheese

1 fresh jalapeño chilli, sliced thinly

2 green onions, sliced thinly

1 Combine beef, stock, the water, chipotle chilli,
bacon, brown onion, garlic, paste, beans, puree
and spices in a 4.5-litre (18-cup) slow cooker. Cook,
covered, on low, for 8 hours. Season to taste.
2 Stir chocolate into the cooker; season to taste.
Serve beef topped with cheese, jalapeño chilli and
green onion.

tips Chipotle chillies in adobo sauce and
mexican chocolate are available from specialist
delicatessens and grocers. If chipotle in adobo
is unavailable use 2-3 tablespoons hot mexican-
style chilli sauce (adding enough to suit your
taste). If the mexican chocolate is unavailable
use dark (semi-sweet) chocolate. If fresh
jalapeño chillies are unavailable, use slices of
bottled pickled jalapeño. Manchego is an aged,
hard, intensely flavoured Spanish cheese. It
is available from Spanish delicatessens and
specialist cheese shops; substitute haloumi
or fetta if not available.
freezing: all versions are suitable to freeze.

nutritional count per serving
- ▶ 42.7g total fat
- ▶ 17g saturated fat
- ▶ 3503kJ (838 cal)
- ▶ 30.3g carbohydrate
- ▶ 78.9g protein
- ▶ 9.6g fibre

mexican beef chilli mole

PREP + COOK TIME 2½ HOURS SERVES 4

2 tablespoons olive oil

1kg (2 pounds) beef chuck steak, cut into 3cm (1¼-inch) pieces

4 rindless bacon slices (260g), chopped coarsely

1 medium brown onion (150g), chopped finely

4 cloves garlic, crushed

3 chipotle peppers in adobo sauce, chopped finely

2 teaspoons each ground cumin, coriander and sweet smoked paprika

¼ teaspoon chilli powder

½ teaspoon ground cinnamon

1½ cups (375ml) beef stock

410g (13 ounces) tomato puree

1 cup (250ml) water

2 tablespoons tomato paste

439g (14 ounces) canned black beans, rinsed, drained

2 tablespoons finely grated mexican chocolate

⅔ cup (80g) grated manchego cheese

1 fresh jalapeño chilli, sliced thinly

2 green onions, sliced thinly

1 Preheat oven to 180°C/350°F.

2 Heat half the oil in a large flameproof casserole dish over high heat on the stove top; cook beef, in batches, until browned. Remove from dish.

3 Heat remaining oil in dish; cook bacon, brown onion and garlic, stirring, until browned lightly. Add chipotle peppers and spices; cook, stirring, for 1 minute or until fragrant.

4 Return beef to dish with stock, puree, the water and paste; bring to the boil. Cover dish, transfer to oven; cook for 1½ hours. Uncover, add beans; return to oven. Cook for 15 minutes or until beef is tender and sauce has thickened.

5 Stir chocolate into dish; season to taste. Serve beef topped with cheese, chilli and green onion.

ON THE STOVE TOP

mexican beef chilli mole

PREP + COOK TIME 2¾ HOURS SERVES 4

2 tablespoons olive oil

1kg (2 pounds) beef chuck steak, cut into 3cm (1¼-inch) pieces

4 rindless bacon slices (260g), chopped coarsely

1 medium brown onion (150g), chopped finely

4 cloves garlic, crushed

3 chipotle peppers in adobo sauce, chopped finely

2 teaspoons each ground cumin, coriander and sweet smoked paprika

¼ teaspoon chilli powder

½ teaspoon ground cinnamon

1½ cups (375ml) beef stock

410g (13 ounces) tomato puree

1 cup (250ml) water

2 tablespoons tomato paste

439g (14 ounces) canned black beans, rinsed, drained

2 tablespoons finely grated mexican chocolate

⅔ cup (80g) grated manchego cheese

1 fresh jalapeño chilli, sliced thinly

2 green onions, sliced thinly

1 Heat half the oil in a large saucepan over high heat; cook beef, in batches, until browned. Remove from pan.

2 Heat remaining oil in pan; cook bacon, brown onion and garlic, stirring, until browned lightly. Add chipotle peppers and spices; cook, stirring, for 1 minute or until fragrant.

3 Return beef to pan with stock, puree, the water and paste; bring to the boil. Reduce heat; simmer, covered, for 1½ hours. Uncover, add beans; simmer, uncovered, for 30 minutes or until beef is tender and sauce has thickened.

4 Stir chocolate into pan; season to taste. Serve beef topped with cheese, chilli and green onion.

LAMB

IN THE SLOW COOKER

lamb shanks
with lentils and pancetta

PREP + COOK TIME 8¾ HOURS SERVES 4

1½ cups (300g) french-style green lentils

4 french-trimmed lamb shanks (800g)

200g (6½ ounces) bottled caramelised onions

2 medium carrots (240g), cut into
1cm (½-inch) pieces

2 stalks celery (300g), cut into
1cm (½-inch) pieces

2 cloves garlic, crushed

100g (3 ounces) thinly sliced pancetta,
chopped coarsely

¼ cup (70g) tomato paste

3 cups (750ml) chicken stock

½ cup (125ml) dry white wine

½ cup (60g) frozen peas

⅓ cup coarsely chopped fresh flat-leaf parsley

1 Rinse lentils under cold water; drain.
2 Combine lentils, lamb, caramelised onion,
carrot, celery, garlic, pancetta, paste, stock and
wine in a 5-litre (20-cup) slow cooker. Cook,
covered, on low, for 8 hours.
3 Add peas to cooker; cook, covered, a further
10 minutes. Season to taste. Sprinkle with parsley
to serve.

freezing: all versions are unsuitable to freeze.

nutritional count per serving
► 22.4g total fat
► 6.2g saturated fat
► 2370kJ (567 cal)
► 46.2g carbohydrate
► 39.4g protein
► 5.3g fibre

lamb shanks with lentils and pancetta

PREP + COOK TIME **4 HOURS** SERVES **4**

2 tablespoons olive oil

4 french-trimmed lamb shanks (800g)

100g (3 ounces) thinly sliced pancetta, chopped coarsely

2 medium carrots (240g), cut into 1cm (½-inch) pieces

2 stalks celery (300g), cut into 1cm (½-inch) pieces

2 cloves garlic, crushed

¼ cup (70g) tomato paste

½ cup (125ml) dry white wine

200g (6½ ounces) bottled caramelised onions

1 litre (4 cups) chicken stock

1½ cups (300g) french-style green lentils

½ cup (60g) frozen peas

⅓ cup coarsely chopped fresh flat-leaf parsley

1 Heat half the oil in a large saucepan over high heat; cook lamb, in batches, until browned. Remove from pan.

2 Heat remaining oil in pan over low heat; cook pancetta, stirring, until browned. Add carrot and celery; cook, stirring, for 1 minute. Add garlic and paste; cook, stirring, for 1 minute. Add wine; bring to the boil. Boil, uncovered, for 1 minute.

3 Return lamb to pan with caramelised onions and stock; bring to the boil. Reduce heat; simmer, covered, for 2½ hours.

4 Meanwhile, rinse lentils under cold water; drain. Add lentils to pan; simmer, uncovered, stirring occasionally, for 40 minutes or until lentils and lamb are tender. Add peas; simmer, uncovered, for 5 minutes or until peas are tender. Season to taste. Serve sprinkled with parsley.

IN THE OVEN

lamb shanks with lentils and pancetta

PREP + COOK TIME **4 HOURS** · SERVES 4

2 tablespoons olive oil

4 french-trimmed lamb shanks (800g)

100g (3 ounces) thinly sliced pancetta, chopped coarsely

2 medium carrots (240g), cut into 1cm (½-inch) pieces

2 stalks celery (300g), cut into 1cm (½-inch) pieces

2 cloves garlic, crushed

¼ cup (70g) tomato paste

½ cup (125ml) dry white wine

200g (6½ ounces) bottled caramelised onions

1 litre (4 cups) chicken stock

1½ cups (300g) french-style green lentils

½ cup (60g) frozen peas

⅓ cup coarsely chopped fresh flat-leaf parsley

1 Preheat oven to 200°C/400°F.

2 Heat half the oil in a large flameproof casserole dish over high heat on the stove top; cook lamb, in batches, until browned. Remove from dish.

3 Heat remaining oil in dish over low heat; cook pancetta, stirring, until browned. Add carrot and celery; cook, stirring, for 1 minute. Add garlic and paste; cook, stirring, for 1 minute. Add wine; bring to the boil. Boil, uncovered, for 1 minute.

4 Return lamb to dish, add caramelised onions and stock; bring to the boil. Cover dish, transfer to oven; cook for 2½ hours.

5 Meanwhile, rinse lentils under cold water; drain. Add lentils to dish, cover; return to oven. Cook for 40 minutes or until lentils and lamb are tender, stirring halfway through cooking time.

6 Add peas to dish; stand, covered, for 5 minutes or until peas are tender. Season to taste. Serve sprinkled with parsley.

spinach

canned diced tomatoes

ground almonds

brown onion

kumara (orange sweet potato)

ground cumin

coconut milk

slivered almonds

garam masala

diced boneless lamb leg

garlic

coriander (cilantro)

long red chilli

lamb, kumara & almond curry

nutritional count per serving
▶ 71g total fat
▶ 31.9g saturated fat
▶ 4443kJ (1063 cal)
▶ 31.8g carbohydrate
▶ 72.2g protein
▶ 7.2g fibre

IN THE OVEN

lamb, kumara & almond curry

PREP + COOK TIME 3½ HOURS SERVES 4

2 tablespoons vegetable oil

1.2kg (2.5 pounds) boneless lamb leg, cut into 5cm (2-inch) pieces

1 large brown onion (200g), sliced thinly

3 cloves garlic, crushed

1 fresh long red chilli, chopped finely

2 teaspoons each garam masala and ground cumin

1 cup (250ml) chicken stock

400g (12½ ounces) canned diced tomatoes

400ml can coconut milk; reserve 2 tablespoons

800g (1½ pounds) kumara (orange sweet potato), cut into 5cm (2-inch) pieces

250g (8 ounces) spinach, trimmed, shredded coarsely

½ cup (60g) ground almonds

⅓ cup (45g) toasted slivered almonds

⅓ cup loosely packed fresh coriander leaves (cilantro)

1 Preheat oven to 180°C/350°F.

2 Heat half the oil in a large flameproof casserole dish over high heat on the stove top; cook lamb, in batches, until browned. Remove from dish.

3 Heat remaining oil in dish over low heat; cook onion, garlic and chilli, stirring, until onion softens. Add spices; cook, stirring, for 1 minute or until fragrant. Return lamb to dish with stock, tomatoes and coconut milk; bring to the boil.

4 Cover dish, transfer to oven; cook for 1¼ hours.

5 Add kumara to dish, cover; return to oven. Cook for 45 minutes or until lamb and kumara are tender.

6 Add spinach and ground nuts to dish; simmer, uncovered, on stove top, until spinach wilts. Season to taste. Drizzle curry with reserved coconut milk, and sprinkle with slivered nuts and coriander, to serve. Accompany with lime wedges, if you like.

serving suggestion Steamed basmati rice
freezing: all versions are unsuitable to freeze.

IN THE SLOW COOKER

lamb, kumara & almond curry

PREP + COOK TIME 8¾ HOURS **SERVES** 4

1.2kg (2.5 pounds) boneless lamb leg, cut into 5cm (2-inch) pieces

800g (1½ pounds) kumara (orange sweet potato), cut into 5cm (2-inch) pieces

1 large brown onion (200g), sliced thinly

3 cloves garlic, crushed

1 fresh long red chilli, chopped finely

2 teaspoons each garam masala and ground cumin

400g (12½ ounces) canned diced tomatoes

400ml can coconut milk; reserve 2 tablespoons

250g (8 ounces) spinach, trimmed, shredded coarsely

½ cup (60g) ground almonds

⅓ cup (45g) toasted slivered almonds

⅓ cup loosely packed fresh coriander leaves (cilantro)

1 Combine lamb, kumara, onion, garlic, chilli, spices, tomatoes and coconut milk in a 5-litre (20-cup) slow cooker. Cook, covered, on low, for 8 hours.
2 Add spinach and ground nuts to cooker; cook, uncovered, on high, for 5 minutes or until spinach wilts. Season to taste. To serve, drizzle curry with reserved coconut milk, and sprinkle with slivered nuts and coriander.

ON THE STOVE TOP

lamb, kumara & almond curry

PREP + COOK TIME 3¼ HOURS **SERVES** 4

2 tablespoons vegetable oil

1.2kg (2.5 pounds) boneless lamb leg, cut into 5cm (2-inch) pieces

1 large brown onion (200g), sliced thinly

3 cloves garlic, crushed

1 fresh long red chilli, chopped finely

2 teaspoons each garam masala and ground cumin

1 cup (250ml) chicken stock

400g (12½ ounces) canned diced tomatoes

400ml can coconut milk; reserve 2 tablespoons

800g (1½ pounds) kumara (orange sweet potato), cut into 5cm (2-inch) pieces

250g (8 ounces) spinach, trimmed, shredded coarsely

½ cup (60g) ground almonds

⅓ cup (45g) toasted slivered almonds

⅓ cup loosely packed fresh coriander leaves (cilantro)

1 Heat half the oil in a large saucepan over high heat; cook lamb, in batches, until browned. Remove from pan. Heat remaining oil in pan over low heat; cook onion, garlic and chilli, stirring, until onion softens. Add spices; cook, stirring, for 1 minute or until fragrant. Return lamb to pan with stock, tomatoes and coconut milk; bring to the boil. Reduce heat; simmer, covered, for 1¼ hours.
2 Add kumara to pan; simmer, covered, for 30 minutes or until lamb and kumara are tender.
3 Add spinach and ground nuts to pan; simmer, uncovered, until spinach wilts. Season to taste. Drizzle curry with reserved coconut milk, and sprinkle with slivered nuts and coriander, to serve.

IN THE SLOW COOKER

moroccan lamb with honey

PREP + COOK TIME 8¾ HOURS **SERVES** 4

400g (12½ ounces) baby carrots, trimmed

600g (1¼ pounds) baby new potatoes

8 spring onions (200g), trimmed

1 cup (250ml) chicken stock

1.5kg (3-pound) lamb shoulder

2 tablespoons honey

2 tablespoons vegetable oil

3 cloves garlic, crushed

2 teaspoons fennel seeds

1 teaspoon each ground cinnamon, ginger and cumin

¼ teaspoon cayenne pepper

1 Combine carrots, potatoes, onions and stock in the base of a 5-litre (20-cup) slow cooker. Score lamb all over at 2.5cm (1-inch) intervals. Combine honey, oil, garlic, seeds and spices in a small bowl. Rub honey mixture all over lamb. Place lamb on top of vegetables in cooker. Cook, covered, on low, for 8 hours.

2 Coarsely shred or slice lamb; serve with vegetables and some of the cooking liquid.

serving suggestion Steamed green beans
freezing: all versions are unsuitable to freeze.

nutritional count per serving
▶ 25.6g total fat
▶ 8.7g saturated fat
▶ 2663kJ (637 cal)
▶ 37.1g carbohydrate
▶ 60.7g protein
▶ 7g fibre

IN THE OVEN

moroccan lamb with honey

PREP + COOK TIME 4 HOURS **SERVES** 4

1.5kg (3-pound) lamb shoulder

2 tablespoons honey

2 tablespoons vegetable oil

3 cloves garlic, crushed

2 teaspoons fennel seeds

1 teaspoon each ground cinnamon, ginger and cumin

¼ teaspoon cayenne pepper

400g (12½ ounces) baby carrots, trimmed

600g (1¼ pounds) baby new potatoes

8 spring onions (200g), trimmed

1 cup (250ml) chicken stock

1 Preheat oven to 180°C/350°F.

2 Score lamb all over at 2.5cm (1-inch) intervals. Combine honey, oil, garlic, seeds and spices in a small bowl. Rub honey mixture all over lamb. Cook lamb in a heated oiled large flameproof baking dish, over high heat, on stove top, until browned all over. Remove from dish.

3 Add carrots, potatoes, onions and stock to dish. Place lamb on top of vegetables; bring to the boil.

4 Cover dish, transfer to oven; cook for 3½ hours or until lamb is very tender.

5 Coarsely shred or slice lamb; serve with vegetables and some of the cooking liquid.

ON THE STOVE TOP

moroccan lamb with honey

PREP + COOK TIME 3½ HOURS **SERVES** 4

1.5kg (3-pound) lamb shoulder

2 tablespoons honey

2 tablespoons vegetable oil

3 cloves garlic, crushed

2 teaspoons fennel seeds

1 teaspoon each ground cinnamon, ginger and cumin

¼ teaspoon cayenne pepper

400g (12½ ounces) baby carrots, trimmed

600g (1¼ pounds) baby new potatoes

8 spring onions (200g), trimmed

1 cup (250ml) chicken stock

1 Score lamb all over at 2.5cm (1-inch) intervals. Combine honey, oil, garlic, seeds and spices in a small bowl. Rub honey mixture all over lamb. Cook lamb in a heated oiled large (wide) heavy-based saucepan, over high heat, until browned all over. Remove from pan.

2 Add carrots, potatoes, onions and stock to pan. Place lamb on top of vegetables; bring to the boil. Reduce heat; simmer, covered, for 3 hours or until lamb is very tender.

3 Coarsely shred or slice lamb; serve with vegetables and some of the cooking liquid.

IN THE SLOW COOKER

*added : gentlemens relish
: red wine*

shepherd's pie

PREP + COOK TIME 11 HOURS SERVES 4

3 medium carrots (360g), chopped coarsely

3 stalks celery (450g), trimmed, chopped coarsely

1 large brown onion (200g), chopped coarsely

2 cloves garlic, crushed

4 sprigs fresh thyme

2 sprigs fresh rosemary

¼ cup (70g) tomato paste

2 tablespoons worcestershire sauce

2½ cups (625ml) beef stock

1.5kg (3-pound) lamb shoulder

½ cup (60g) frozen peas

150g (4½ ounces) baby spinach leaves

1 tablespoon cornflour (cornstarch)

1 tablespoon water

800g (1½ pounds) potatoes, chopped coarsely

40g (1½ ounces) butter

½ cup (125ml) hot milk

½ cup (60g) coarsely grated cheddar

1 Combine carrot, celery, onion, garlic, herbs, paste, sauce and stock in a 5-litre (20-cup) slow cooker. Add lamb, turn to coat in mixture. Cook, covered, on high for 2 hours. Reduce to low; cook for 8 hours.

2 Remove lamb from cooker; shred meat coarsely, discard fat and bones. Discard herbs from cooker. Return lamb to cooker with peas and spinach. Blend cornflour and the water in a small cup, stir into the cooker; cook, uncovered, on high, for 20 minutes or until thickened. Season to taste.

3 Meanwhile, boil, steam or microwave potato until tender; drain. Mash potato with butter and hot milk until smooth; season to taste.

4 Preheat grill (broiler).

5 Transfer lamb to a 2.5-litre (10-cup) ovenproof dish. Spoon potato over lamb mixture; sprinkle with cheese. Grill for 5 minutes or until top is browned lightly.

freezing: **all versions are suitable to freeze.**

nutritional count per serving
▶ 40.1g total fat
▶ 18.8g saturated fat
▶ 3160kJ (756 cal)
▶ 26g carbohydrate
▶ 68.6g protein
▶ 8.7g fibre

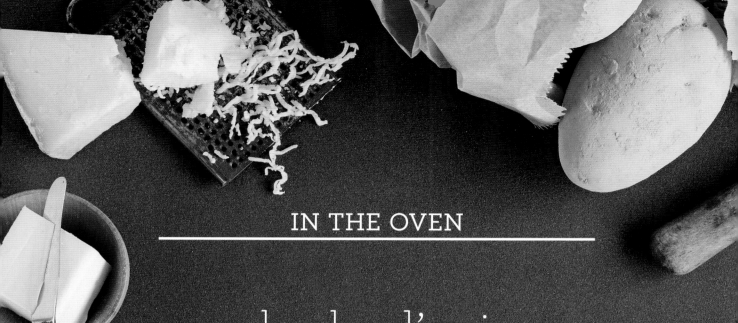

shepherd's pie

PREP + COOK TIME 4 HOURS **SERVES** 4

2 tablespoons olive oil

1.5kg (3-pound) lamb shoulder

3 medium carrots (360g), chopped coarsely

3 stalks celery (450g), trimmed, chopped coarsely

1 large brown onion (200g), chopped coarsely

2 cloves garlic, crushed

¼ cup (70g) tomato paste

4 sprigs fresh thyme

2 sprigs fresh rosemary

2 tablespoons worcestershire sauce

3 cups (750ml) beef stock

½ cup (60g) frozen peas

150g (4½ ounces) baby spinach leaves

800g (1½ pounds) potatoes, chopped coarsely

40g (1½ ounces) butter

½ cup (125ml) hot milk

½ cup (60g) coarsely grated cheddar

1 Preheat oven to 180°C/350°F.

2 Heat half the oil in a large flameproof baking dish over high heat on the stove top; cook lamb, turning, until browned all over. Remove from dish.

3 Heat remaining oil in dish over low heat; cook carrot, celery, onion and garlic, stirring, until onion softens. Add paste; cook, stirring, for 1 minute. Return lamb to dish with herbs, sauce and stock; bring to the boil.

4 Cover dish, transfer to oven; cook for 3 hours or until lamb is very tender and almost falling off the bone.

5 Remove lamb from dish; when cool enough to handle, shred meat coarsely, discard fat and bones. Discard herbs from dish. Return lamb to dish with peas and spinach; simmer, uncovered, until spinach wilts. Season to taste.

6 Meanwhile, boil, steam or microwave potato until tender; drain. Mash potato with butter and hot milk until smooth; season to taste.

7 Preheat grill (broiler).

8 Transfer lamb to a 2.5-litre (10-cup) ovenproof dish. Spoon potato over lamb mixture; sprinkle with cheese. Grill for 5 minutes or until top is browned lightly.

ON THE STOVE TOP

shepherd's pie

PREP + COOK TIME 5 HOURS SERVES 4

2 tablespoons olive oil

1.5kg (3-pound) lamb shoulder

3 medium carrots (360g), chopped coarsely

3 stalks celery (450g), trimmed, chopped coarsely

1 large brown onion (200g), chopped coarsely

2 cloves garlic, crushed

¼ cup (70g) tomato paste

4 sprigs fresh thyme

2 sprigs fresh rosemary

2 tablespoons worcestershire sauce

3 cups (750ml) beef stock

½ cup (60g) frozen peas

150g (4½ ounces) baby spinach leaves

800g (1½ pounds) potatoes, chopped coarsely

40g (1½ ounces) butter

½ cup (125ml) hot milk

½ cup (60g) coarsely grated cheddar

1 Heat half the oil in a large (wide) saucepan over high heat; cook lamb, turning, until browned all over. Remove from pan.

2 Heat remaining oil in pan over low heat; cook carrot, celery, onion and garlic, stirring, until onion softens. Add paste; cook, stirring, for 1 minute. Return lamb to pan with herbs, sauce and stock; bring to the boil. Reduce heat; simmer, covered, for 4 hours or until lamb is very tender and almost falling off the bone.

3 Remove lamb from pan; when cool enough to handle, shred meat coarsely, discard fat and bones. Discard herbs from pan. Return lamb to pan with peas and spinach; simmer, uncovered, until spinach wilts. Season to taste.

4 Meanwhile, boil, steam or microwave potato until tender; drain. Mash potato with butter and hot milk until smooth; season to taste.

5 Preheat grill (broiler).

6 Transfer lamb to a 2.5-litre (10-cup) ovenproof dish. Spoon potato over lamb mixture; sprinkle with cheese. Grill for 5 minutes or until top is browned lightly.

IN THE SLOW COOKER

sun-dried tomato and balsamic lamb stew

PREP + COOK TIME 8¾ HOURS SERVES 4

8 lamb neck chops (1.4kg)

400g (12½ ounces) canned diced tomatoes

1 medium red onion (170g), sliced thinly

2 cloves garlic, crushed

1 cup (250ml) beef stock

½ cup (125ml) dry red wine

⅓ cup (80ml) balsamic vinegar

½ cup (75g) coarsely chopped sun-dried tomatoes

¼ cup loosely packed fresh basil leaves

2 sprigs fresh thyme

340g (11-ounce) jar marinated artichoke hearts, drained

2 teaspoons cornflour (cornstarch)

1 tablespoon water

¼ cup loosely packed fresh baby basil leaves, extra

1 Combine lamb, tomatoes, onion, garlic, stock, wine, vinegar, sun-dried tomatoes and herbs in a 5-litre (20-cup) slow cooker. Cook, covered, on low, for 8 hours.

2 Discard thyme from cooker; stir in artichokes. Combine cornflour with the water in a small cup; stir into cooker. Cook, covered, on high, for 10 minutes or until thickened slightly. Season to taste.

3 Serve stew sprinkled with extra basil.

tip We used red wine but you can use white wine if you prefer.
serving suggestion Creamy polenta or mashed potato.
freezing: all versions are suitable to freeze.

nutritional count per serving
▶ 71.1g total fat
▶ 29.7g saturated fat
▶ 3958kJ (947 cal)
▶ 18g carbohydrate
▶ 52.2g protein
▶ 7.2g fibre

sun-dried tomato and balsamic lamb stew

PREP + COOK TIME 2½ HOURS SERVES 4

2 tablespoons plain (all-purpose) flour

8 lamb neck chops (1.4kg)

2 tablespoons olive oil

1 medium red onion (170g), sliced thinly

2 cloves garlic, crushed

½ cup (125ml) dry red wine

⅓ cup (80ml) balsamic vinegar

2 cups (500ml) beef stock

400g (12½ ounces) canned diced tomatoes

½ cup (75g) coarsely chopped sun-dried tomatoes

¼ cup loosely packed fresh basil leaves

2 sprigs fresh thyme

340g (11-ounce) jar marinated artichoke hearts, drained

¼ cup loosely packed fresh baby basil leaves, extra

1 Preheat oven to 160°C/325°F.

2 Season flour in a large bowl; dust lamb in flour, shake off excess (reserve remaining flour in bowl). Heat half the oil in a large flameproof casserole dish over medium-high heat on the stove top; cook lamb, in batches, until browned. Remove from pan.

3 Heat remaining oil in dish over low heat on stove top; cook onion and garlic, stirring, until onion is soft. Add reserved flour; cook, stirring, for 1 minute.

4 Gradually add wine to dish; bring to the boil. Add vinegar, stock, tomatoes, sun-dried tomatoes and herbs. Return lamb to dish; bring to the boil.

5 Cover dish, transfer to oven; cook for 2 hours or until lamb is tender and almost falling off the bone.

6 Discard thyme; stir in artichokes. Simmer, on stove top, until heated through. Season to taste. Serve sprinkled with extra basil.

ON THE STOVE TOP

sun-dried tomato and balsamic lamb stew

PREP + COOK TIME 2 HOURS SERVES 4

2 tablespoons plain (all-purpose) flour

8 lamb neck chops (1.4kg)

2 tablespoons olive oil

1 medium red onion (170g), sliced thinly

2 cloves garlic, crushed

½ cup (125ml) dry red wine

⅓ cup (80ml) balsamic vinegar

2 cups (500ml) beef stock

400g (12½ ounces) canned diced tomatoes

½ cup (75g) coarsely chopped sun-dried tomatoes

¼ cup loosely packed fresh basil leaves

2 sprigs fresh thyme

340g (11-ounce) jar marinated artichoke hearts, drained

¼ cup loosely packed fresh baby basil leaves, extra

1 Season flour in a large bowl; dust lamb in flour, shake off excess (reserve remaining flour in bowl). Heat half the oil in a large saucepan over medium-high heat; cook lamb, in batches, until browned. Remove from pan.

2 Heat remaining oil in pan over low heat; cook onion and garlic, stirring, until onion softens. Add reserved flour; cook, stirring, for 1 minute. Gradually add wine; bring to the boil.

3 Add vinegar, stock, tomatoes, sun-dried tomatoes and herbs to pan. Return lamb to pan; bring to the boil. Reduce heat; simmer, covered, for 1½ hours or until lamb is tender and almost falling off the bone.

4 Discard thyme; stir in artichokes. Simmer, uncovered, until heated through. Season to taste. Serve sprinkled with extra basil.

IN THE SLOW COOKER

lamb shanks & eggplant stew

PREP + COOK TIME 10¾ HOURS SERVES 4

4 french-trimmed lamb shanks (1kg)

2 medium eggplants (600g), chopped coarsely

1 medium red onion (170g), sliced thinly

2 stalks celery (300g), trimmed, sliced thinly

3 cloves garlic, sliced thinly

700g (1½ pounds) passata

2 cups (500ml) beef stock

1 cup (250ml) water

⅔ cup (80g) pitted green olives

2 tablespoons rinsed, drained baby capers

2 tablespoons dried currants

1½ tablespoons red wine vinegar

½ cup loosely packed fresh basil leaves, torn

1 Place lamb shanks in the base of a 4.5-litre (18-cup) slow cooker. Top with eggplant, onion, celery, garlic and passata. Pour over stock and the water. Cook, covered, on low, for 10 hours. Season to taste.

2 Carefully remove lamb shanks. Skim excess fat from stew. Stir in olives, capers, currants, vinegar and basil. Serve lamb shanks with olive mixture; sprinkle with extra basil leaves, if you like.

tips Make sure the lamb goes in on the base of the slow cooker as this prevents the vegetables from becoming too soft. Passata is sieved tomato puree and is available from most supermarkets.
serving suggestion Creamy polenta and wilted greens; accompany with garlic and herb-rubbed bread.
freezing: all versions are suitable to freeze.

nutritional count per serving
► 26.4g total fat
► 7.7g saturated fat
► 1956kJ (468 cal)
► 18.6g carbohydrate
► 34g protein
► 9.5g fibre

IN THE OVEN

lamb shanks & eggplant stew

PREP + COOK TIME 2¾ HOURS SERVES 4

2 tablespoons olive oil

4 french-trimmed lamb shanks (1kg)

2 medium eggplants (600g), chopped coarsely

1 medium red onion (170g), sliced thinly

2 stalks celery (300g), trimmed, sliced thinly

3 cloves garlic, sliced thinly

2 x 400g (13-ounce) cans diced tomatoes

2 cups (500ml) beef stock

⅔ cup (80g) pitted green olives

2 tablespoons rinsed, drained baby capers

2 tablespoons dried currants

1½ tablespoons red wine vinegar

½ cup loosely packed fresh basil leaves, torn

1 Preheat oven to 180°C/350°F.
2 Heat half the oil in a large flameproof casserole dish over high heat on the stove top; cook lamb until browned all over. Remove from pan.
3 Heat remaining oil in dish; cook eggplant, onion, celery and garlic, stirring, for 10 minutes or until vegetables are softened.
4 Return lamb to pan with tomatoes and stock; bring to the boil. Cover dish, transfer to oven; cook for 1¾ hours. Uncover, return to oven; cook for 20 minutes or until lamb is falling off the bone and sauce has thickened.
5 Stir olives, capers, currants, vinegar and basil into stew; season to taste. Serve lamb topped with extra basil leaves, if you like.

ON THE STOVE TOP

lamb shanks & eggplant stew

PREP + COOK TIME 3¼ HOURS SERVES 4

2 tablespoons olive oil

4 french-trimmed lamb shanks (1kg)

2 medium eggplants (600g), chopped coarsely

1 medium red onion (170g), sliced thinly

2 stalks celery (300g), trimmed, sliced thinly

3 cloves garlic, sliced thinly

2 x 400g (13-ounce) cans diced tomatoes

2 cups (500ml) beef stock

⅔ cup (80g) pitted green olives

2 tablespoons rinsed, drained baby capers

2 tablespoons dried currants

1½ tablespoons red wine vinegar

½ cup loosely packed fresh basil leaves, torn

1 Heat half the oil in a large saucepan over high heat; cook lamb until browned all over. Remove from pan.
2 Heat remaining oil in pan; cook eggplant, onion, celery and garlic, stirring, for 10 minutes or until vegetables are softened.
3 Return lamb to pan with tomatoes and stock; bring to the boil. Reduce heat; simmer, covered, for 2 hours. Uncover; simmer a further 30 minutes or until lamb is falling off the bone and sauce has thickened.
4 Stir olives, capers, currants, vinegar and basil into stew; season to taste. Serve lamb topped with extra basil leaves, if you like.

IN THE SLOW COOKER

sicilian meatballs in spicy tomato sauce

PREP + COOK TIME 8¾ HOURS SERVES 4

700g (1½ pounds) bottled passata

410g (13 ounces) canned crushed tomatoes

1 medium brown onion (150g), chopped finely

45g (1½ ounces) canned anchovies, drained

¼ teaspoon dried chilli flakes

3 cloves garlic, sliced thinly

1 cup (250ml) chicken stock

2 cups (500ml) water

⅓ cup fresh oregano leaves, torn

600g (1¼ pounds) minced (ground) lamb

1 cup (70g) stale breadcrumbs

2 tablespoons pine nuts, chopped coarsely

1 tablespoon finely grated lemon rind

¼ cup (40g) sultanas, chopped coarsely

¼ cup (20g) finely grated parmesan

⅓ cup loosely packed small fresh basil leaves

1 Place passata, tomatoes, onion, anchovies, chilli, garlic, stock, the water and half the oregano in a 4.5-litre (18-cup) slow cooker. Stir to combine.
2 Using hand, combine lamb, breadcrumbs, nuts, rind, sultanas, parmesan and remaining oregano in a large bowl; roll level tablespoons of mixture into balls. Transfer to cooker. Cook, covered, on low, for 8 hours. Season to taste. Serve sprinkled with basil.

tip Passata is sieved tomato puree available from most supermarkets.
serving suggestion Cooked pasta, creamy polenta or mashed potato.
freezing: all versions are suitable to freeze. Uncooked meatballs and sauce can be frozen separately, then cooked at a later stage.

62

nutritional count per serving
▶ 34.4g total fat
▶ 10.8g saturated fat
▶ 2642kJ (632 cal)
▶ 33.4g carbohydrate
▶ 44g protein
▶ 4.3g fibre

sicilian meatballs
in spicy tomato sauce

PREP + COOK TIME **55 MINUTES** SERVES **4**

600g (1¼ pounds) minced (ground) lamb

1 cup (70g) stale breadcrumbs

2 tablespoons pine nuts, chopped coarsely

1 tablespoon finely grated lemon rind

¼ cup (40g) sultanas, chopped coarsely

¼ cup (20g) finely grated parmesan

⅓ cup fresh oregano leaves, torn

1 tablespoon olive oil

1 medium brown onion (150g), chopped finely

45g (1½ ounces) canned anchovies, drained

¼ teaspoon dried chilli flakes

3 cloves garlic, sliced thinly

700g (1½ pounds) bottled passata

410g (13 ounces) canned crushed tomatoes

1 cup (250ml) chicken stock

⅓ cup loosely packed small fresh basil leaves

1 Preheat oven to 180°C/350°F.
2 Using hand, combine lamb, breadcrumbs, nuts, rind, sultanas, parmesan and half the oregano in a large bowl; roll level tablespoons of mixture into balls.
3 Heat oil in a large shallow flameproof casserole dish over high heat on the stove top; cook onion, anchovies, chilli and garlic, stirring, until softened. Add passata, tomatoes and stock; bring to the boil. Reduce heat; simmer, uncovered, for 5 minutes.
4 Add meatballs to dish; transfer to oven. Cook, uncovered, for 20 minutes or until meatballs are cooked through and sauce has thickened. Serve sprinkled with basil and remaining oregano.

tip Try topping baked meatballs with slices of bocconcini or crumbled fetta for the last 5 minutes of the cooking time.

ON THE STOVE TOP

sicilian meatballs in spicy tomato sauce

PREP + COOK TIME 50 MINUTES SERVES 4

600g (1¼ pounds) minced (ground) lamb

1 cup (70g) stale breadcrumbs

2 tablespoons pine nuts, chopped coarsely

1 tablespoon finely grated lemon rind

¼ cup (40g) sultanas, chopped coarsely

¼ cup (20g) finely grated parmesan

⅓ cup fresh oregano leaves, torn

1 tablespoon olive oil

1 medium brown onion (150g), chopped finely

45g (1½ ounces) canned anchovies, drained

¼ teaspoon dried chilli flakes

3 cloves garlic, sliced thinly

700g (1½ pounds) bottled passata

410g (13 ounces) canned crushed tomatoes

1 cup (250ml) chicken stock

⅓ cup loosely packed small fresh basil leaves

1 Using hand, combine lamb, breadcrumbs, nuts, rind, sultanas, parmesan and half the oregano in a large bowl; roll level tablespoons of mixture into balls.

2 Heat oil in a large shallow saucepan over high heat; cook onion, anchovies, chilli and garlic, stirring, until softened. Add passata, tomatoes and stock; bring to the boil. Reduce heat; simmer, uncovered, 5 minutes.

3 Add meatballs to pan; simmer, uncovered, for 15 minutes or until meatballs are cooked through and sauce has thickened. Serve sprinkled with basil and remaining oregano.

ginger

brown onion

canned crushed tomatoes

lamb rump steaks

thyme sprigs

chicken stock

mexican chilli powder

garlic

dried oregano

ground cumin

coriander (cilantro)

ground cloves

fresh bay leaves

seeded prunes

whole roasted piquillo peppers

ground cinnamon

lamb birria

nutritional count per serving
- ▶ 17.6g total fat
- ▶ 4.1g saturated fat
- ▶ 1722kJ (412 cal)
- ▶ 18.2g carbohydrate
- ▶ 42.6g protein
- ▶ 4.4g fibre

IN THE SLOW COOKER

lamb birria
(spicy mexican lamb stew)

PREP + COOK TIME 10¾ HOURS **SERVES** 4

3 teaspoons mexican chilli powder

1 teaspoon dried oregano

1 teaspoon ground cumin

¼ teaspoon each ground cloves and cinnamon

4 teaspoons finely grated fresh ginger

3 cloves garlic, sliced thinly

700g (1½ pounds) trimmed lamb rump steaks, cut into 3cm (1¼-inch) cubes

2 sprigs fresh thyme

2 fresh bay leaves

2 cups (500ml) salt-reduced chicken stock

1 cup (250ml) water

1 medium brown onion (150g), chopped coarsely

285g (9-ounce) jar whole roasted piquillo peppers, drained, chopped coarsely

410g (13 ounces) canned crushed tomatoes

½ cup (85g) seeded prunes, halved

½ cup loosely packed fresh coriander leaves (cilantro)

1 Place chilli powder, oregano, cumin, cloves, cinnamon, ginger and garlic in a 4.5-litre (18-cup) slow cooker. Add lamb; toss to coat in mixture.

2 Add thyme, bay leaves, stock, the water, onion, peppers and tomatoes. Cook, covered, on low, for 10 hours. Season to taste.

3 Remove and discard thyme and bay leaves. Stir in prunes. Cook, covered, on low, for 10 minutes or until prunes soften. Serve topped with coriander.

serving suggestion Grilled corn tortillas and lime wedges.
freezing: all versions are suitable to freeze.

68

ON THE STOVE TOP

lamb birria

PREP + COOK TIME 2¾ HOURS SERVES 4

2 tablespoons olive oil

700g (1½ pounds) trimmed lamb rump steaks, cut into 3cm (1¼-inch) cubes

1 medium brown onion (150g), chopped coarsely

4 teaspoons finely grated fresh ginger

3 cloves garlic, sliced thinly

3 teaspoons mexican chilli powder

1 teaspoon dried oregano

1 teaspoon ground cumin

¼ teaspoon each ground cloves and cinnamon

2 sprigs fresh thyme

2 fresh bay leaves

285g (9-ounce) jar whole roasted piquillo peppers, drained, chopped coarsely

410g (13 ounces) canned crushed tomatoes

2 cups (500ml) salt-reduced chicken stock

1 cup (250ml) water

½ cup (85g) seeded prunes, halved

½ cup loosely packed fresh coriander leaves (cilantro)

1 Heat half the oil in a large saucepan over high heat; cook lamb, in batches, until browned. Remove from pan.

2 Heat remaining oil in pan; cook onion, ginger and garlic, stirring, until softened. Add chilli powder, oregano, cumin, cloves and cinnamon; cook, stirring, for 1 minute or until fragrant.

3 Return lamb to pan with thyme, bay leaves, peppers, tomatoes, stock and the water; bring to the boil. Reduce heat; simmer, covered, for 1½ hours. Uncover; add prunes, simmer for 20 minutes or until lamb is tender and sauce has thickened.

4 Discard thyme and bay leaves. Season; serve lamb topped with coriander.

IN THE OVEN

lamb birria

PREP + COOK TIME 2¾ HOURS SERVES 4

2 tablespoons olive oil

700g (1½ pounds) trimmed lamb rump steaks, cut into 3cm (1¼-inch) cubes

1 medium brown onion (150g), chopped coarsely

4 teaspoons finely grated fresh ginger

3 cloves garlic, sliced thinly

3 teaspoons mexican chilli powder

1 teaspoon dried oregano

1 teaspoon ground cumin

¼ teaspoon each ground cloves and cinnamon

2 sprigs fresh thyme

2 fresh bay leaves

285g (9-ounce) jar whole roasted piquillo peppers, drained, chopped coarsely

410g (13 ounces) canned crushed tomatoes

2 cups (500ml) salt-reduced chicken stock

1 cup (250ml) water

½ cup (85g) seeded prunes, halved

½ cup loosely packed fresh coriander leaves (cilantro)

1 Preheat oven to 180°C/350°F. Heat half the oil in a large flameproof casserole dish over high heat on stove top; cook lamb, in batches, until browned. Remove lamb from dish.

2 Heat remaining oil in dish; cook onion, ginger and garlic, stirring, until softened. Add chilli powder, oregano, cumin, cloves and cinnamon; cook, stirring, for 1 minute or until fragrant.

3 Return lamb to dish with thyme, bay leaves, peppers, tomatoes, stock and the water; bring to the boil. Cover, transfer to oven; cook for 1½ hours. Uncover, add prunes; return to oven; cook for 15 minutes or until lamb is tender and sauce has thickened.

4 Discard thyme and bay leaves. Season; serve lamb topped with coriander.

CHICKEN

IN THE SLOW COOKER

country-style chicken stew

PREP + COOK TIME 8¾ HOURS SERVES 4

1.4kg (2¾-pound) whole chicken

1 medium leek (350g), sliced into 1cm (½-inch) thick rounds

2 celery stalks (300g), trimmed, cut into 5cm (2-inch) lengths

400g (12½ ounces) baby carrots, trimmed

6 shallots (150g), halved

4 fresh thyme sprigs

2 fresh bay leaves

2 fresh flat-leaf parsley stalks

1½ litres (6 cups) salt-reduced chicken stock

2 cups (500ml) water

50g (1½ ounces) angel hair pasta, broken in half

150g (4 ½ ounces) green beans, halved lengthways

1½ tablespoons lemon juice

⅓ cup coarsely chopped fresh flat-leaf parsley

1 Place chicken, leek, celery, carrots, shallot, thyme, bay leaves, parsley stalks, stock and the water in a 4.5-litre (18-cup) slow cooker. Cook, covered, on low, for 8 hours. Carefully remove chicken from cooker. Discard bay leaves, thyme and parsley stalks. Skim excess fat from stew.
2 Add pasta and beans to cooker. Cook, covered, on high, for 12 minutes or until pasta and beans are tender. Season to taste.
3 Meanwhile, discard skin from chicken. Break chicken into large pieces (drumstick, thigh, breast etc). Divide chicken into serving bowls.
4 Stir juice and chopped parsley into stew. To serve, spoon vegetables, pasta and broth over chicken.

freezing: all versions are unsuitable to freeze.

nutritional count per serving
▶ 29.9g total fat
▶ 8.7g saturated fat
▶ 2161kJ (517 cal)
▶ 20.2g carbohydrate
▶ 38.5g protein
▶ 8.1g fibre

country-style chicken stew

PREP + COOK TIME 1¾ HOURS SERVES 4

1 tablespoon olive oil

4 skinless chicken drumsticks (520g)

4 skinless chicken thigh cutlets (800g)

1 medium leek (350g), sliced into 1cm (½-inch) thick rounds

2 celery stalks (300g), trimmed, cut into 5cm (2-inch) lengths

400g (12½ ounces) baby carrots, trimmed

6 shallots (150g), halved

4 fresh thyme sprigs

2 fresh bay leaves

2 fresh flat-leaf parsley stalks

1½ litres (6 cups) salt-reduced chicken stock

150g (4½ ounces) green beans, halved lengthways

50g (1½ ounces) angel hair pasta, broken in half

1½ tablespoons lemon juice

⅓ cup coarsely chopped fresh flat-leaf parsley

1 Preheat oven to 180°C/350°F.

2 Heat oil in a large flameproof casserole dish over medium-high heat on the stove top; cook chicken, in batches, turning, until browned all over. Return chicken to dish.

3 Add leek, celery, carrots, shallot, thyme, bay leaves, parsley stalks and stock; bring to the boil. Cover, transfer to oven; cook for 1 hour.

4 Uncover; add beans and pasta to dish. Return dish to oven; cook for 3 minutes or until pasta is tender. Stir in juice and chopped parsley; season to taste.

ON THE STOVE TOP

country-style chicken stew

PREP + COOK TIME 1½ HOURS SERVES 4

1 tablespoon olive oil

4 skinless chicken drumsticks (520g)

4 skinless chicken thigh cutlets (800g)

1 medium leek (350g), sliced into 1cm
(½-inch) thick rounds

2 celery stalks (300g), trimmed, cut into
5cm (2-inch) lengths

400g (12½ ounces) baby carrots, trimmed

6 shallots (150g), halved

4 fresh thyme sprigs

2 fresh bay leaves

2 fresh flat-leaf parsley stalks

1½ litres (6 cups) salt-reduced chicken stock

150g (4½ ounces) green beans, halved lengthways

50g (1½ ounces) angel hair pasta, broken in half

1½ tablespoons lemon juice

⅓ cup coarsely chopped fresh flat-leaf parsley

1 Heat oil in a large saucepan over medium-high heat; cook chicken, in batches, turning, until browned all over. Return chicken to pan.
2 Add leek, celery, carrots, shallot, thyme, bay leaves, parsley stalks and stock to pan; bring to the boil. Reduce heat; simmer, uncovered, for 1 hour or until chicken is cooked through and liquid reduces.
3 Add beans and pasta to pan; bring to the boil. Reduce heat; simmer, uncovered, for 3 minutes or until pasta is tender. Stir in juice and chopped parsley; season to taste.

IN THE SLOW COOKER

cock-a-leekie soup

PREP + COOK TIME 9 HOURS SERVES 6

1.2kg (2½-pound) whole chicken

2 cloves garlic, sliced thinly

4 medium leeks (1.4kg), sliced thinly

2 stalks celery (300g), trimmed, sliced thinly

4 sprigs fresh thyme

large pinch cayenne pepper

2½ litres (10 cups) salt-reduced chicken stock

1 cup (170g) seeded prunes

2 tablespoons coarsely chopped fresh oregano

2 tablespoons coarsely chopped fresh flat-leaf parsley

1 Place chicken, garlic, leek, celery, thyme, cayenne pepper and 2 litres stock in a 4.5-litre (18-cup) slow cooker. Cook, covered, on low, for 8 hours.

2 Carefully remove chicken from cooker; discard bones and skin. Shred meat coarsely using two forks.

3 Return chicken to cooker with prunes and remaining stock. Cook, covered, on high, for 30 minutes or until prunes soften and stock is hot. Discard thyme; season to taste.

4 Stir oregano and parsley into soup to serve.

serving suggestion Mini scones or soda bread.
freezing: all versions are suitable to freeze.

nutritional count per serving
- ▶ 14.3g total fat
- ▶ 4.3g saturated fat
- ▶ 1363kJ (326 cal)
- ▶ 20.6g carbohydrate
- ▶ 26.4g protein
- ▶ 7.4g fibre

IN THE OVEN

cock-a-leekie soup

PREP + COOK TIME 1½ HOURS **SERVES** 6

1.2kg (2½-pound) whole chicken

2 cloves garlic, sliced thinly

4 medium leeks (1.4kg), sliced thinly

2 stalks celery (300g), trimmed, sliced thinly

4 sprigs fresh thyme

large pinch cayenne pepper

2½ litres (10 cups) salt-reduced chicken stock

1 cup (170g) seeded prunes

2 tablespoons coarsely chopped fresh oregano

2 tablespoons coarsely chopped fresh flat-leaf parsley

1 Preheat oven to 180°C/350°F.
2 Place chicken, garlic, leek, celery, thyme, cayenne pepper and stock in a large flameproof casserole dish over medium-high heat on the stove top; bring to the boil. Cover dish, transfer to oven; cook for 40 minutes or until chicken is cooked through.
3 Uncover; carefully remove chicken from dish. Add prunes; return dish to oven. Cook for 15 minutes or until prunes soften and stock is hot.
4 Meanwhile, discard skin and bones from chicken; shred meat coarsely using two forks.
5 Discard thyme; season to taste. Stir chicken, oregano and parsley into soup to serve.

ON THE STOVE TOP

cock-a-leekie soup

PREP + COOK TIME 1¼ HOURS (+ STANDING) **SERVES** 6

1.2kg (2½-pound) whole chicken

2 cloves garlic, sliced thinly

4 medium leeks (1.4kg), sliced thinly

2 stalks celery (300g), trimmed, sliced thinly

4 sprigs fresh thyme

large pinch cayenne pepper

2½ litres (10 cups) salt-reduced chicken stock

1 cup (170g) seeded prunes

2 tablespoons coarsely chopped fresh oregano

2 tablespoons coarsely chopped fresh flat-leaf parsley

1 Place chicken, garlic, leek, celery, thyme, cayenne pepper and stock in a large saucepan over medium-high heat; bring to the boil. Reduce heat; simmer, covered, for 30 minutes or until chicken is almost cooked through. Cover, stand for 30 minutes.
2 Carefully remove chicken from pan; discard skin and bones from chicken. Shred meat coarsely using two forks.
3 Return chicken to pan with prunes; bring to the boil. Reduce heat; simmer, uncovered, for 10 minutes or until prunes soften and stock is hot.
4 Discard thyme; season to taste. Stir oregano and parsley into soup to serve.

IN THE SLOW COOKER

chicken and mushroom soup

PREP + COOK TIME 10½ HOURS SERVES 4

1.2kg (2½-pound) whole boiler hen

1 medium brown onion (150g) chopped coarsely

2 cloves garlic, crushed

300g (9½ ounces) swiss brown mushrooms, halved

300g (9½ ounces) button mushrooms, halved

10g (½ ounce) dried porcini mushrooms

1 stalk celery (150g), trimmed, chopped coarsely

2 medium potatoes (400g), chopped coarsely

1 litre (4 cups) water

2 cups (500ml) chicken stock

300ml pouring cream

⅓ cup loosely packed fresh chervil leaves

1 Rinse chicken under cold water; pat dry, inside and out, with absorbent paper. Trim excess fat from chicken; place chicken in a 5-litre (20-cup) slow cooker. Add onion, garlic, fresh and dried mushrooms, celery, potato, the water and stock. Cook, covered, on low, for 10 hours.

2 Remove chicken from cooker; when cool enough to handle, discard skin and bones. Shred chicken meat coarsely.

3 Using a stick blender, blend soup in cooker until smooth; stir in cream and shredded chicken meat. Cook, covered, on high, for 10 minutes or until hot. Season to taste. Serve soup sprinkled with chervil and drizzle with a little extra cream, if you like.

note Boiler hens, also known as steamer hens or steamer chickens, are usually 'older' birds used for egg-laying – the meat is generally tougher, making them more suitable for slow-cooked soups like this one. They are available from specialty chicken shops or ordered from the butcher. You can use a small 'young/meat' chicken if you cannot find a boiler; however, you will need to reduce the cooking time from 10 hours to 8 hours on low.
freezing: all versions are unsuitable to freeze.

nutritional count per serving
▶ 51.4g total fat
▶ 27.1g saturated fat
▶ 2964kJ (709 cal)
▶ 17.5g carbohydrate
▶ 42g protein
▶ 6.9g fibre

chicken and mushroom soup

PREP + COOK TIME 3¾ HOURS SERVES 4

1.2kg (2½-pound) whole boiler hen

1 medium brown onion (150g) chopped coarsely

2 cloves garlic, crushed

10g (½ ounce) dried porcini mushrooms

1 stalk celery (150g), trimmed, chopped coarsely

1 litre (4 cups) water

2 cups (500ml) chicken stock

300g (9½ ounces) swiss brown mushrooms, halved

300g (9½ ounces) button mushrooms, halved

2 medium potatoes (400g), chopped coarsely

300ml pouring cream

⅓ cup loosely packed fresh chervil leaves

1 Preheat oven to 180°C/350°F.

2 Rinse chicken under cold water; pat dry, inside and out, with absorbent paper. Trim excess fat from chicken. Place chicken in a large flameproof casserole dish with onion, garlic, dried mushrooms, celery, the water and stock; bring to the boil on stove top.

3 Cover dish, transfer to oven; cook for 2 hours.

4 Add fresh mushrooms and potato to dish; cover, return to oven. Cook for 1 hour or until chicken is tender.

5 Remove chicken from dish; when cool enough to handle, discard skin and bones. Shred chicken meat coarsely.

6 Using a stick blender, blend soup in dish until smooth; stir in cream and shredded chicken meat. Simmer, uncovered, until hot; season to taste. Serve soup sprinkled with chervil and drizzle with a little extra cream, if you like.

ON THE STOVE TOP

chicken and mushroom soup

PREP + COOK TIME 3¾ HOURS SERVES 4

1.2kg (2½-pound) whole boiler hen

1 medium brown onion (150g) chopped coarsely

2 cloves garlic, crushed

10g (½ ounce) dried porcini mushrooms

1 stalk celery (150g), trimmed, chopped coarsely

1 litre (4 cups) water

2 cups (500ml) chicken stock

300g (9½ ounces) swiss brown mushrooms, halved

300g (9½ ounces) button mushrooms, halved

2 medium potatoes (400g), chopped coarsely

300ml pouring cream

⅓ cup loosely packed fresh chervil leaves

1 Rinse chicken under cold water; pat dry, inside and out, with absorbent paper. Trim excess fat from chicken. Place chicken in a large saucepan with onion, garlic, dried mushrooms, celery, the water and stock; bring to the boil. Reduce heat; simmer, covered, for 2 hours.

2 Add fresh mushrooms and potato to pan; simmer, covered, for 1 hour or until chicken is tender.

3 Remove chicken from pan; when cool enough to handle, discard skin and bones. Shred chicken meat coarsely.

4 Using a stick blender, blend soup in pan until smooth; stir in cream and shredded chicken meat. Simmer, uncovered, until hot; season to taste. Serve soup sprinkled with chervil and drizzle with a little extra cream, if you like.

IN THE SLOW COOKER

shredded mexican chicken and beans

PREP + COOK TIME 8¾ HOURS SERVES 4

1.6kg (3¼-pound) whole chicken

800g (1½ pounds) canned kidney beans, rinsed, drained

1 medium brown onion (150g), sliced thinly

3 cloves garlic, crushed

1 medium red capsicum (bell pepper) (200g), chopped coarsely

1 medium green capsicum (bell pepper) (200g), chopped coarsely

1 corn cob (250g), trimmed, kernels removed

2 tablespoons tomato paste

400g (12½ ounces) canned diced tomatoes

1 cup (250ml) chicken stock

2 teaspoons each ground cumin and dried oregano

1 teaspoon each smoked paprika and dried chilli flakes

½ cup loosely packed fresh coriander (cilantro)

8 flour tortillas (400g)

AVOCADO SALSA

1 large avocado (320g), chopped coarsely

1 lebanese cucumber (130g), chopped coarsely

125g (4 ounces) cherry tomatoes, quartered

1 tablespoon lime juice

1 green onion (scallion), sliced thinly

1 Rinse chicken under cold water; pat dry, inside and out, with absorbent paper. Trim excess fat from chicken.

2 Combine beans, onion, garlic, capsicums, corn kernels, paste, tomatoes, stock and spices in a 5-litre (20-cup) slow cooker. Place chicken in cooker, push down into bean mixture. Cook, covered, on low, for 8 hours.

3 Remove chicken from cooker; when cool enough to handle, discard skin and bones. Shred chicken meat coarsely.

4 Return meat to cooker; cook, covered, on low, for 20 minutes or until hot. Season to taste.

5 Meanwhile, make avocado salsa. Sprinkle chicken mixture with coriander; serve with avocado salsa and tortillas. Accompany with sour cream, if you like.

avocado salsa Combine ingredients in a small bowl; season to taste.

tip You can use 250g (8 ounces) of frozen corn kernels, or a rinsed and drained 400g (12½-ounce) can of corn kernels instead of the fresh kernels, if you prefer.

freezing: all versions are suitable to freeze.

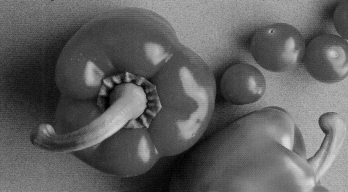

nutritional count per serving
▶ 51.6g total fat
▶ 15.5g saturated fat
▶ 4665kJ (1116 cal)
▶ 87.2g carbohydrate
▶ 65.2g protein
▶ 18g fibre

shredded mexican chicken and beans

PREP + COOK TIME 2¼ HOURS SERVES 4

1.6kg (3¼-pound) whole chicken

1 tablespoon olive oil

1 medium brown onion (150g), sliced thinly

3 cloves garlic, crushed

1 medium red capsicum (bell pepper) (200g), chopped coarsely

1 medium green capsicum (bell pepper) (200g), chopped coarsely

1 corn cob (250g), trimmed, kernels removed

2 tablespoons tomato paste

2 teaspoons each ground cumin and dried oregano

1 teaspoon each smoked paprika and dried chilli flakes

400g (12½ ounces) canned diced tomatoes

1½ cups (375ml) chicken stock

800g (1½ pounds) canned kidney beans, rinsed, drained

½ cup loosely packed fresh coriander (cilantro)

8 flour tortillas (400g)

AVOCADO SALSA

1 large avocado (320g), chopped coarsely

1 lebanese cucumber (130g), chopped coarsely

125g (4 ounces) cherry tomatoes, quartered

1 tablespoon lime juice

1 green onion (scallion), sliced thinly

1 Preheat oven to 180°C/350°F.

2 Rinse chicken under cold water; pat dry, inside and out, with absorbent paper. Trim excess fat from chicken.

3 Heat oil in a large flameproof casserole dish, over low heat, on the stove top; cook onion and garlic, stirring, until onion softens. Add capsicums, corn kernels, paste and spices; cook, stirring, for 2 minutes or until fragrant. Add tomatoes and stock to the dish, then add chicken; turn to coat chicken in mixture. Bring to the boil.

4 Cover dish, transfer to oven; cook for 1½ hours.

5 Remove chicken from dish; when cool enough to handle, discard skin and bones. Shred chicken meat coarsely.

6 Return meat to dish with beans; bring to the boil. Remove from heat; season to taste.

7 Meanwhile, make avocado salsa. Sprinkle chicken mixture with coriander; serve with avocado salsa and tortillas. Accompany with sour cream, if you like.

avocado salsa Combine ingredients in a small bowl; season to taste.

ON THE STOVE TOP

shredded mexican chicken and beans

PREP + COOK TIME 2¼ HOURS SERVES 4

1.6kg (3¼-pound) whole chicken

1 tablespoon olive oil

1 medium brown onion (150g), sliced thinly

3 cloves garlic, crushed

1 medium red capsicum (bell pepper) (200g), chopped coarsely

1 medium green capsicum (bell pepper) (200g), chopped coarsely

1 corn cob (250g), trimmed, kernels removed

2 tablespoons tomato paste

2 teaspoons each ground cumin and dried oregano

1 teaspoon each smoked paprika and dried chilli flakes

400g (12½ ounces) canned diced tomatoes

2 cups (500ml) chicken stock

800g (1½ pounds) canned kidney beans, rinsed, drained

½ cup loosely packed fresh coriander (cilantro)

8 flour tortillas (400g)

AVOCADO SALSA

1 large avocado (320g), chopped coarsely

1 lebanese cucumber (130g), chopped coarsely

125g (4 ounces) cherry tomatoes, quartered

1 tablespoon lime juice

1 green onion (scallion), sliced thinly

1 Rinse chicken under cold water; pat dry, inside and out, with absorbent paper. Trim excess fat from chicken.

2 Heat oil in a large saucepan over low heat; cook onion and garlic, stirring, until onion softens. Add capsicums, corn kernels, paste and spices; cook, stirring, for 2 minutes or until fragrant. Add tomatoes and stock to the dish, then add chicken; turn to coat chicken in mixture. Bring to the boil, reduce heat; simmer, covered, for 1½ hours.

3 Remove chicken from pan; when cool enough to handle, discard skin and bones. Shred chicken meat coarsely.

4 Return meat to pan with beans; bring to the boil. Remove from heat; season to taste.

5 Meanwhile, make avocado salsa. Sprinkle chicken mixture with coriander; serve with avocado salsa and tortillas. Accompany with sour cream, if you like.

avocado salsa Combine ingredients in a small bowl; season to taste.

PORK

IN THE SLOW COOKER

soy pork with mushrooms

PREP + COOK TIME 8½ HOURS **SERVES** 4

1.2kg (2½ pounds) boneless pork shoulder

2 cinnamon sticks

2 star anise

⅔ cup (160ml) soy sauce

½ cup (125ml) chinese cooking wine

¼ cup (55g) firmly packed brown sugar

1 fresh long red chilli, halved lengthways

25g (¾ ounce) fresh ginger, sliced thinly

6 cloves garlic, bruised

2½ cups (625ml) water

150g (4½ ounces) shiitake mushrooms, halved if large

150g (4½ ounces) oyster mushrooms, torn into large pieces

150g (4½ ounces) shimeji mushrooms

100g (3 ounces) enoki mushrooms

4 baby buk choy, halved or quartered

1 Place pork, cinnamon, star anise, sauce, cooking wine, sugar, chilli, ginger, garlic and the water in a 4.5-litre (18-cup) slow cooker. Cook, covered, on low, for 8 hours.

2 Carefully remove pork from cooker; stand, covered, for 15 minutes. Using a slotted spoon, remove cinnamon, star anise, chilli, ginger and garlic from broth.

3 Add mushrooms and buk choy to cooker. Cook, covered, on high, for 15 minutes or until mushrooms are tender; season to taste. Serve slices of pork with vegetables and a little broth. Accompany with rice noodles, if you like.

tip When adding the mushrooms and buk choy, don't worry if they aren't covered by the broth. They will shrink slightly whilst cooking. Place the buk choy on top of the mushrooms as this will ensure it stays green.

freezing: all versions are unsuitable to freeze.

nutritional count per serving
▶ 4.5g total fat
▶ 1.2g saturated fat
▶ 2011kJ (481 cal)
▶ 17.8g carbohydrate
▶ 78.5g protein
▶ 12.3g fibre

IN THE OVEN

soy pork with mushrooms

PREP + COOK TIME 3 HOURS **SERVES** 4

1.2kg (2½ pounds) boneless pork shoulder

2 cinnamon sticks

2 star anise

⅔ cup (160ml) soy sauce

½ cup (125ml) chinese cooking wine

¼ cup (55g) firmly packed brown sugar

1 fresh long red chilli, halved lengthways

25g (¾ ounce) fresh ginger, sliced thinly

6 cloves garlic, bruised

3 cups (750ml) water

150g (4½ ounces) shiitake mushrooms, halved if large

150g (4½ ounces) oyster mushrooms, torn into large pieces

150g (4½ ounces) shimeji mushrooms

100g (3 ounces) enoki mushrooms

4 baby buk choy, halved or quartered

1 Preheat oven to 180°C/350°F.
2 Place pork, cinnamon, star anise, sauce, cooking wine, sugar, chilli, ginger, garlic and the water in a large flameproof casserole dish; bring to the boil on the stove top. Cover dish, transfer to oven; cook for 2¼ hours.
3 Increase oven temperature to 220°C/425°F.
4 Uncover; add mushrooms to dish. Return to oven; cook, uncovered, for 20 minutes or until pork is very tender. Add buk choy to dish; cook, uncovered, for 5 minutes or until tender.
5 Slice pork; serve with vegetables and a little of the broth.

ON THE STOVE TOP

soy pork with mushrooms

PREP + COOK TIME 2¾ HOURS **SERVES** 4

1.2kg (2½ pounds) boneless pork shoulder

2 cinnamon sticks

2 star anise

⅔ cup (160ml) soy sauce

½ cup (125ml) chinese cooking wine

¼ cup (55g) firmly packed brown sugar

1 fresh long red chilli, halved lengthways

25g (¾ ounce) fresh ginger, sliced thinly

6 cloves garlic, bruised

3 cups (750ml) water

150g (4½ ounces) shiitake mushrooms, halved if large

150g (4½ ounces) oyster mushrooms, torn into large pieces

150g (4½ ounces) shimeji mushrooms

100g (3 ounces) enoki mushrooms

4 baby buk choy, halved or quartered

1 Place pork, cinnamon, star anise, sauce, cooking wine, sugar, chilli, ginger, garlic and the water in a large saucepan over high heat; bring to the boil. Reduce heat; simmer, covered, for 2¼ hours or until pork is very tender.
2 Add mushrooms to pan; cook, uncovered, for 15 minutes. Add buk choy to pan; cook, uncovered, for 5 minutes or until tender.
3 Slice pork; serve with vegetables and a little of the broth.

IN THE SLOW COOKER

red pork and lychee curry

PREP + COOK TIME 8½ HOURS SERVES 4

565g (1¼ pounds) canned seeded lychees in syrup

1.5kg (3 pounds) pork belly ribs (spare ribs), rind removed, halved

1 large brown onion (200g), sliced thinly

2 cloves garlic, crushed

⅓ cup (100g) red curry paste

400ml canned coconut milk

½ cup (125ml) chicken stock

2 fresh kaffir lime leaves

2 tablespoons fish sauce

227g (7 ounces) canned water chestnut slices, rinsed, drained

125g (4 ounces) baby corn, halved

400g (12½ ounces) baby carrots, trimmed

200g (6½ ounces) snow peas, trimmed

⅓ cup (25g) fried shallots

⅓ cup loosely packed fresh coriander leaves (cilantro)

2 limes, cut into wedges

1 Drain lychees over a medium bowl; reserve ⅓ cup syrup and lychees separately. Refrigerate reserved lychees.

2 Combine reserved syrup, pork, onion, garlic, curry paste, coconut milk, stock, kaffir lime leaves, sauce, water chestnut, corn and carrots in a 5-litre (20-cup) slow cooker. Cook, covered, on low, for 8 hours.

3 Discard lime leaves. Add lychees and snow peas to cooker; cook, uncovered, on high, for 5 minutes or until snow peas are tender. Season to taste. Serve curry sprinkled with shallots and coriander; accompany with lime wedges.

tip Fried shallots are often found on Asian tables and are used as a condiment or sprinkled over cooked dishes. They are available, canned or in cellophane bags, at Asian grocery stores; once opened, leftovers will keep for months if tightly sealed. Make your own by thinly slicing shallots and shallow-frying in vegetable oil until golden-brown and crisp.

serving suggestion Steamed jasmine rice.

freezing: all versions are unsuitable to freeze.

nutritional count per serving
▶ 66.4g total fat
▶ 31.4g saturated fat
▶ 4523kJ (1082 cal)
▶ 39.8g carbohydrate
▶ 76.6g protein
▶ 14.6g fibre

red pork and lychee curry

PREP + COOK TIME 2½ HOURS SERVES 4

565g (1¼ pounds) canned seeded lychees in syrup

2 tablespoons peanut oil

1.5kg (3 pounds) pork belly ribs (spare ribs), rind removed, halved

1 large brown onion (200g), sliced thinly

2 cloves garlic, crushed

⅓ cup (100g) red curry paste

400ml canned coconut milk

1 cup (250ml) chicken stock

2 fresh kaffir lime leaves

2 tablespoons fish sauce

125g (4 ounces) baby corn, halved

400g (12½ ounces) baby carrots, trimmed

227g (7 ounces) canned water chestnut slices, rinsed, drained

200g (6½ ounces) snow peas, trimmed

⅓ cup (25g) fried shallots

⅓ cup loosely packed fresh coriander leaves (cilantro)

2 limes, cut into wedges

1 Preheat oven to 180°C/350°F.

2 Drain lychees over a medium bowl; reserve ⅓ cup syrup and lychees separately. Refrigerate reserved lychees.

3 Heat half the oil in a large flameproof casserole dish, over high heat, on the stove top; cook pork, in batches, until browned. Remove from dish.

4 Heat remaining oil in dish over low heat; cook onion and garlic, stirring, until onion softens. Add curry paste; cook, stirring, for 2 minutes or until fragrant. Return pork to dish with coconut milk, stock, kaffir lime leaves, sauce and reserved syrup; bring to the boil.

5 Cover dish, transfer to oven; cook for 1 hour. Add corn and carrots; cover, return to oven. Cook for 30 minutes or until pork and vegetables are tender.

6 Discard lime leaves. Add reserved lychees, water chestnut and snow peas to dish; simmer, uncovered, on stove top, for 5 minutes or until snow peas are tender. Season to taste. Serve curry sprinkled with shallots and coriander; accompany with lime wedges.

ON THE STOVE TOP

red pork and lychee curry

PREP + COOK TIME 2½ HOURS SERVES 4

565g (1¼ pounds) canned seeded lychees in syrup

2 tablespoons peanut oil

1.5kg (3 pounds) pork belly ribs (spare ribs), rind removed, halved

1 large brown onion (200g), sliced thinly

2 cloves garlic, crushed

⅓ cup (100g) red curry paste

400ml canned coconut milk

1 cup (250ml) chicken stock

2 fresh kaffir lime leaves

2 tablespoons fish sauce

125g (4 ounces) baby corn, halved

400g (12½ ounces) baby carrots, trimmed

227g (7 ounces) canned water chestnut slices, rinsed, drained

200g (6½ ounces) snow peas, trimmed

⅓ cup (25g) fried shallots

⅓ cup loosely packed fresh coriander leaves (cilantro)

2 limes, cut into wedges

1 Drain lychees over a medium bowl; reserve ⅓ cup syrup and lychees separately. Refrigerate reserved lychees.

2 Heat half the oil in a large saucepan over high heat; cook pork, in batches, until browned. Remove from pan.

3 Heat remaining oil in pan over low heat; cook onion and garlic, stirring, until onion softens. Add curry paste; cook, stirring, for 2 minutes or until fragrant. Return pork to pan with coconut milk, stock, kaffir lime leaves, sauce and reserved syrup; bring to the boil. Reduce heat, simmer, covered, for 1 hour. Add corn and carrots; simmer, covered, for 30 minutes or until pork and vegetables are tender.

4 Discard lime leaves. Add reserved lychees, water chestnut and snow peas to pan; simmer, uncovered, for 5 minutes or until snow peas are tender. Season to taste. Serve curry sprinkled with shallots and coriander; accompany with lime wedges.

canned crushed tomatoes

brown onion

chicken stock

brown sugar

dijon mustard

hot chilli sauce

golden syrup

speck

flat-leaf parsley

worcestershire sauce

borlotti beans

butter beans

cannellini beans

94

nutritional count per serving
▶ 17.2g total fat
▶ 5.2g saturated fat
▶ 2291kJ (548 cal)
▶ 63.7g carbohydrate
▶ 30.3g protein
▶ 9.7g fibre

IN THE SLOW COOKER

boston baked beans

PREP + COOK TIME 10½ HOURS **SERVES** 4

1 large brown onion (200g), chopped finely

300g (9½-ounce) piece speck, rind removed, chopped finely

¼ cup (90g) golden syrup (or treacle)

⅓ cup (75g) firmly packed brown sugar

2 tablespoons dijon mustard

1 tablespoon worcestershire sauce

1 tablespoon hot chilli sauce

410g (13 ounces) canned crushed tomatoes

400g (12½ ounces) canned cannellini beans, rinsed, drained

400g (12½ ounces) canned butter beans, rinsed, drained

400g (12½ ounces) canned borlotti beans, rinsed, drained

3 cups (750ml) salt-reduced chicken stock

½ cup finely chopped fresh flat-leaf parsley

1 Place onion, speck, syrup, sugar, mustard, sauces, tomatoes, beans and stock in a 4.5-litre (18-cup) slow cooker. Cook, covered, on low, for 9 hours. Uncover, cook, on low, for 1 hour or until thickened slightly. Season to taste.
2 Stir in half the parsley. Serve sprinkled with remaining parsley.

serving suggestion Baby spinach leaves and crusty bread.
freezing: all versions are suitable to freeze before adding the parsley (add the parsley after reheating).

IN THE OVEN

boston baked beans

PREP + COOK TIME 1¾ HOURS **SERVES** 4

1 tablespoon olive oil

1 large brown onion (200g), chopped finely

300g (9½-ounce) piece speck, rind removed, chopped finely

¼ cup (90g) golden syrup (or treacle)

⅓ cup (75g) firmly packed brown sugar

2 tablespoons dijon mustard

1 tablespoon worcestershire sauce

1 tablespoon hot chilli sauce

410g (13 ounces) canned crushed tomatoes

400g (12½ ounces) canned cannellini beans, rinsed, drained

400g (12½ ounces) canned butter beans, rinsed, drained

400g (12½ ounces) canned borlotti beans, rinsed, drained

2 cups (500ml) salt-reduced chicken stock

½ cup finely chopped fresh flat-leaf parsley

1 Preheat oven to 180°C/350°F.
2 Heat oil in a large flameproof casserole dish, over medium-high heat, on the stove top; cook onion and speck, stirring, for 10 minutes or until browned lightly.
3 Add syrup, sugar, mustard, sauces, tomatoes, beans and stock; bring to the boil. Cover dish, transfer to oven; cook for 1¼ hours or until sauce thickens. Stir in parsley.

ON THE STOVE TOP

boston baked beans

PREP + COOK TIME 45 MINUTES **SERVES** 4

1 tablespoon olive oil

1 large brown onion (200g), chopped finely

300g (9½-ounce) piece speck, rind removed, chopped finely

¼ cup (90g) golden syrup (or treacle)

⅓ cup (75g) firmly packed brown sugar

2 tablespoons dijon mustard

1 tablespoon worcestershire sauce

1 tablespoon hot chilli sauce

410g (13 ounces) canned crushed tomatoes

2 tablespoons tomato paste

400g (12½ ounces) canned cannellini beans, rinsed, drained

400g (12½ ounces) canned butter beans, rinsed, drained

400g (12½ ounces) canned borlotti beans, rinsed, drained

1½ cups (375ml) salt-reduced chicken stock

½ cup finely chopped fresh flat-leaf parsley

1 Heat oil in a large saucepan over medium-high heat; cook onion and speck, stirring, for 10 minutes or until browned lightly.
2 Add syrup, sugar, mustard, sauces, tomatoes, paste, beans and stock; bring to the boil. Reduce heat; simmer, uncovered, for 25 minutes or until sauce thickens. Stir in parsley.

IN THE OVEN

peppered pork curry

PREP + COOK TIME 2¼ HOURS SERVES 4

2 tablespoons vegetable oil or ghee

1.2kg (2½ pounds) diced boneless pork shoulder

1 medium red onion (170g), sliced thinly

4 cloves garlic, crushed

4 teaspoons finely grated fresh ginger

2 teaspoons cracked black pepper

2 teaspoons ground cumin

1 teaspoon ground fenugreek

½ teaspoon ground cardamom

1 cinnamon stick

1 cup (250ml) chicken stock

400g (12½ ounces) canned diced tomatoes

2 tablespoons brown sugar

1 cup (280g) thick greek-style yoghurt

150g (4½ ounces) baby spinach leaves

⅓ cup loosely packed fresh coriander leaves (cilantro)

1 Preheat oven to 180°C/350°F.

2 Heat half the oil in a large flameproof casserole dish over high heat on the stove top; cook pork, in batches, until browned. Remove from dish.

3 Heat remaining oil in dish over low heat; cook onion, garlic and ginger, stirring, until onion softens. Add spices; cook, stirring, for 1 minute or until fragrant. Return pork to dish with stock, tomatoes, sugar and half the yoghurt; bring to the boil.

4 Cover dish, transfer to oven; cook for 1½ hours or until pork is tender.

5 Discard cinnamon. Add spinach and remaining yoghurt; simmer, uncovered, on stove top, until spinach wilts. Season to taste. Serve curry sprinkled with coriander; top with extra yoghurt, if you like.

serving suggestion Steamed rice and warmed roti bread.
freezing: all versions are suitable to freeze.

nutritional count per serving
- ▶ 17.6g total fat
- ▶ 5.2g saturated fat
- ▶ 2278kJ (545 cal)
- ▶ 21.8g carbohydrate
- ▶ 72.3g protein
- ▶ 3.6g fibre

IN THE SLOW COOKER

peppered pork curry

PREP + COOK TIME 8½ HOURS SERVES 4

1.2kg (2½ pounds) diced boneless pork shoulder

1 medium red onion (170g), sliced thinly

4 cloves garlic, crushed

4 teaspoons finely grated fresh ginger

2 tablespoons brown sugar

2 teaspoons cracked black pepper

1 cinnamon stick

2 teaspoons ground cumin

1 teaspoon ground fenugreek

½ teaspoon ground cardamom

1 cup (250ml) chicken stock

400g (12½ ounces) canned diced tomatoes

1 cup (280g) thick greek-style yoghurt

150g (4½ ounces) baby spinach leaves

⅓ cup loosely packed fresh coriander leaves (cilantro)

1 Combine pork, onion, garlic, ginger, sugar, spices, stock, tomatoes and half the yoghurt in a 5-litre (20-cup) slow cooker. Cook, covered, on low, for 8 hours.

2 Discard cinnamon. Add spinach and remaining yoghurt to cooker; cook, uncovered, on high, for 5 minutes or until spinach wilts. Season to taste. Serve curry sprinkled with coriander; top with extra yoghurt, if you like.

ON THE STOVE TOP

peppered pork curry

PREP + COOK TIME 2¼ HOURS SERVES 4

2 tablespoons vegetable oil or ghee

1.2kg (2½ pounds) diced boneless pork shoulder

1 medium red onion (170g), sliced thinly

4 cloves garlic, crushed

4 teaspoons finely grated fresh ginger

2 teaspoons cracked black pepper

2 teaspoons ground cumin

1 teaspoon ground fenugreek

½ teaspoon ground cardamom

1 cinnamon stick

1 cup (250ml) chicken stock

400g (12½ ounces) canned diced tomatoes

2 tablespoons brown sugar

1 cup (280g) thick greek-style yoghurt

150g (4½ ounces) baby spinach leaves

⅓ cup loosely packed fresh coriander leaves (cilantro)

1 Heat half the oil in a large saucepan over high heat; cook pork, in batches, until browned. Remove from pan.

2 Heat remaining oil in pan over low heat; cook onion, garlic and ginger, stirring, until onion softens. Add spices; cook, stirring, for 1 minute or until fragrant. Return pork to pan with stock, tomatoes, sugar and half the yoghurt; bring to the boil. Reduce heat; simmer, covered, for 1½ hours or until pork is tender.

3 Discard cinnamon. Add spinach and remaining yoghurt to pan; simmer, uncovered, until spinach wilts. Season to taste. Serve curry sprinkled with coriander; top with extra yoghurt, if you like.

VEGETABLE

IN THE SLOW COOKER

split pea and capsicum curry

added cumin
Geebas Rogan Josh
curry paste x2 @ 30g.

PREP + COOK TIME 8½ HOURS SERVES 4

1 medium brown onion (150g), sliced thinly

500g (1 pound) baby new potatoes, halved

1 large carrot (180g), halved, sliced thickly

1 medium red capsicum (bell pepper) (350g), chopped coarsely

1 medium yellow capsicum (bell pepper) (350g), chopped coarsely

⅓ cup (100g) mild indian curry paste

⅓ cup (85g) yellow split peas

⅓ cup (85g) green split peas

8 fresh curry leaves

2 tablespoons tomato paste

410g (13 ounces) canned crushed tomatoes

2 cups (500ml) vegetable stock

2 cups (500ml) water

150g (4½ ounces) sugar snap peas

1 bunch spinach (500g), chopped coarsely

¾ cup (200g) greek-style yoghurt

½ cup loosely packed fresh coriander leaves (cilantro)

1 Place onion, potato, carrot, capsicums, curry paste, split peas, curry leaves, tomato paste, tomatoes, stock and the water in a 4.5-litre (18-cup) slow cooker. Cook, covered, on low, for 8 hours. Season to taste.

2 Stir in sugar snap peas. Cook, uncovered, on low, for 10 minutes or until peas are tender. Stir in spinach. Serve curry topped with yoghurt and sprinkled with coriander.

serving suggestion Steamed rice and pappadums.
freezing: all versions are unsuitable to freeze.

split pea and capsicum curry

PREP + COOK TIME 1¾ HOURS SERVES 4

⅓ cup (85g) yellow split peas

⅓ cup (85g) green split peas

1 tablespoon olive oil

1 medium brown onion (150g), sliced thinly

⅓ cup (100g) mild indian curry paste

2 tablespoons tomato paste

8 fresh curry leaves

500g (1 pound) baby new potatoes, halved

1 large carrot (180g), halved, sliced thickly

1 medium red capsicum (bell pepper) (350g), chopped coarsely

1 medium yellow capsicum (bell pepper) (350g), chopped coarsely

410g (13 ounces) canned crushed tomatoes

2 cups (500ml) vegetable stock

1 cup (250ml) water

150g (4½ ounces) sugar snap peas

1 bunch spinach (500g), chopped coarsely

¾ cup (200g) greek-style yoghurt

½ cup loosely packed fresh coriander leaves (cilantro)

1 Add split peas to a medium saucepan of boiling water; boil, uncovered, for 35 minutes or until tender, drain.

2 Meanwhile, preheat oven to 180°C/350°F.

3 Heat oil in a large flameproof casserole dish, over medium-high heat, on the stove top; cook onion, stirring, until softened. Add pastes and curry leaves; cook, stirring, for 2 minutes or until fragrant.

4 Add potatoes, carrot, capsicums, tomatoes, stock and the water to dish; bring to the boil. Cover dish, transfer to oven; cook for 35 minutes. Uncover; add split peas; cook for a further 35 minutes or until vegetables are tender and sauce has thickened.

5 Add sugar snap peas and spinach to dish; stand, covered, for 5 minutes or until peas are tender. Season to taste. Serve curry topped with yoghurt and coriander.

ON THE STOVE TOP

split pea and capsicum curry

PREP + COOK TIME 1½ HOURS SERVES 4

⅓ cup (85g) yellow split peas

⅓ cup (85g) green split peas

1 tablespoon olive oil

1 medium brown onion (150g), sliced thinly

⅓ cup (100g) mild indian curry paste

2 tablespoons tomato paste

8 fresh curry leaves

500g (1 pound) baby new potatoes, halved

1 large carrot (180g), halved, sliced thickly

1 medium red capsicum (bell pepper) (350g), chopped coarsely

1 medium yellow capsicum (bell pepper) (350g), chopped coarsely

410g (13 ounces) canned crushed tomatoes

2 cups (500ml) vegetable stock

1 cup (250ml) water

150g (4½ ounces) sugar snap peas

1 bunch spinach (500g), chopped coarsely

¾ cup (200g) greek-style yoghurt

½ cup loosely packed fresh coriander leaves (cilantro)

1 Add split peas to a medium saucepan of boiling water; boil, uncovered, for 35 minutes or until tender, drain.

2 Meanwhile, heat oil in a large saucepan over medium-high heat; cook onion, stirring, until softened. Add pastes and curry leaves; cook, stirring, for 2 minutes or until fragrant.

3 Add potatoes, carrot, capsicums, tomatoes, stock and the water to pan; bring to the boil. Reduce heat; simmer, covered, for 30 minutes. Uncover; add split peas, cook for a further 30 minutes or until vegetables are tender and sauce has thickened.

4 Add sugar snap peas and spinach to pan; cook, uncovered, for 3 minutes or until peas are tender. Season to taste. Serve curry topped with yoghurt and coriander.

IN THE SLOW COOKER

spiced carrot & kumara soup

PREP + COOK TIME 9 HOURS **SERVES** 4

2 medium brown onions (300g), chopped coarsely

5 medium carrots (600g), chopped coarsely

3 small kumara (orange sweet potato) (750g), chopped coarsely

1 tablespoon ground coriander

2 teaspoons cumin seeds

½ teaspoon dried chilli flakes

1 litre (4 cups) salt-reduced chicken stock

2 cups (500ml) water

¾ cup (200g) greek-style yoghurt

½ cup firmly packed fresh coriander sprigs (cilantro)

1 Place onion, carrot, kumara, ground coriander, cumin, chilli, stock and the water in a 4.5-litre (18-cup) slow cooker. Cook, covered, on low, for 8 hours.

2 Cool soup 10 minutes. Blend or process soup, in batches, until smooth. Return soup to cooker. Cook, covered, on high, for 20 minutes or until hot. Season to taste.

3 To serve, dollop soup with yoghurt and sprinkle with fresh coriander. Accompany with warm naan bread, if you like.

tip If the soup is a little thick add a little more stock or water. Swap chicken stock for vegetable for a vegetarian option.
freezing: all versions are suitable to freeze.

nutritional count per serving
▶ 13.5g total fat
▶ 3.7g saturated fat
▶ 1396kJ (334 cal)
▶ 39.9g carbohydrate
▶ 8.9g protein
▶ 9.6g fibre

IN THE OVEN

spiced carrot, & kumara soup

PREP + COOK TIME 1¼ HOURS **SERVES** 4

2 tablespoons olive oil

2 medium brown onions (300g), chopped coarsely

5 medium carrots (600g), chopped coarsely

3 small kumara (orange sweet potato) (750g), chopped coarsely

1 tablespoon ground coriander

2 teaspoons cumin seeds

½ teaspoon dried chilli flakes

1 litre (4 cups) salt-reduced chicken stock

2 cups (500ml) water

¾ cup (200g) greek-style yoghurt

½ cup firmly packed fresh coriander sprigs (cilantro)

1 Preheat oven to 180°C/350°F.
2 Heat oil in a large flameproof casserole dish, over medium-high heat, on the stove top; cook onion, carrot and kumara, stirring, until onion softens. Add ground coriander, cumin and chilli, cook, stirring, for 1 minute or until fragrant.
3 Add stock and the water to dish; cover, transfer to oven. Cook for 30 minutes. Uncover; return to oven. Cook for 20 minutes or until vegetables are tender.
4 Cool soup for 10 minutes. Blend soup, in batches, until smooth. Return to dish; stir over medium-high heat, on the stove top, until heated through.
5 To serve, dollop soup with yoghurt and sprinkle with fresh coriander. Accompany with warm naan bread, if you like.

ON THE STOVE TOP

spiced carrot, & kumara soup

PREP + COOK TIME 50 MINUTES **SERVES** 4

2 tablespoons olive oil

2 medium brown onions (300g), chopped coarsely

5 medium carrots (600g), chopped coarsely

3 small kumara (orange sweet potato) (750g), chopped coarsely

1 tablespoon ground coriander

2 teaspoons cumin seeds

½ teaspoon dried chilli flakes

1 litre (4 cups) salt-reduced chicken stock

2 cups (500ml) water

¾ cup (200g) greek-style yoghurt

½ cup firmly packed fresh coriander sprigs (cilantro)

1 Heat oil in a large saucepan over medium-high heat; cook onion, carrot and kumara, stirring, until onion softens. Add ground coriander, cumin and chilli; cook, stirring, for 1 minute or until fragrant.
2 Add stock and the water to pan; bring to the boil. Reduce heat; simmer, covered, for 30 minutes or until vegetables are tender.
3 Cool soup for 10 minutes. Blend soup, in batches, until smooth. Return to pan; stir over medium-high heat until heated through.
4 To serve, dollop soup with yoghurt and sprinkle with fresh coriander. Accompany with warm naan bread, if you like.

IN THE SLOW COOKER

vegetable stew with polenta dumplings

PREP + COOK TIME 9 HOURS SERVES 4

1 medium red onion (170g), cut into wedges

2 medium zucchini (240g), sliced thickly

4 yellow patty pan squash (120g), cut into wedges

1 medium kumara (orange sweet potato) (400g), chopped coarsely

2 medium carrots (240g), chopped coarsely

1 trimmed corn cob (250g), cut into 6 rounds

1 medium red capsicum (bell pepper) (350g), chopped coarsely

2 flat mushrooms (160g) cut into wedges

3 cloves garlic, crushed

30g (1-ounce) sachet taco seasoning

2 teaspoons paprika

2 x 400g (13-ounce) cans crushed tomatoes

1 cup (250ml) vegetable stock

2 tablespoons fresh flat-leaf parsley leaves

POLENTA DUMPLINGS

1 cup (150g) self-raising flour

2 tablespoons polenta (cornmeal)

60g (2 ounces) cold butter, chopped

1 egg, beaten lightly

¼ cup (20g) finely grated parmesan

2 tablespoons milk, approximately

1 Place onion, zucchini, squash, kumara, carrot, corn, capsicum, mushrooms, garlic, seasoning, paprika, tomatoes and stock in a 4.5-litre (18-cup) slow cooker. Cook, covered, on low, for 8 hours.

2 Make polenta dumpling mixture just before required.

3 Drop level tablespoons of dumpling mixture, about 2cm (¾-inch) apart, on top of stew. Cook, covered, on low, for 30 minutes or until dumplings are firm to touch and cooked through. Serve stew with dumplings and sprinkle with parsley leaves.

polenta dumplings Place flour and polenta in a medium bowl; rub in butter. Stir in egg, cheese and enough milk to make a soft, sticky dough.

tip Try adding rinsed, drained canned kidney beans, or trimmed green beans for the last 10 minutes of cooking time.

freezing: all versions are unsuitable to freeze.

nutritional count per serving
- ▶ 22.9g total fat
- ▶ 8g saturated fat
- ▶ 2483kJ (594 cal)
- ▶ 70g carbohydrate
- ▶ 19.4g protein
- ▶ 15.5g fibre

vegetable stew with polenta dumplings

PREP + COOK TIME 1½ HOURS SERVES 4

1 tablespoon olive oil

1 medium red onion (170g), cut into wedges

3 cloves garlic, crushed

30g (1-ounce) sachet taco seasoning

2 teaspoons paprika

2 medium zucchini (240g), sliced thickly

4 yellow patty pan squash (120g), cut into wedges

1 medium kumara (orange sweet potato) (400g), chopped coarsely

2 medium carrots (240g), chopped coarsely

1 trimmed corn cob (250g), cut into 6 rounds

1 medium red capsicum (bell pepper) (350g), chopped coarsely

2 flat mushrooms (160g) cut into wedges

2 x 400g (13 ounces) canned crushed tomatoes

1 cup (250ml) vegetable stock

2 tablespoons fresh flat-leaf parsley leaves

POLENTA DUMPLINGS

1 cup (150g) self-raising flour

2 tablespoons polenta (cornmeal)

60g (2 ounces) cold butter, chopped

1 egg, beaten lightly

¼ cup (20g) finely grated parmesan

2 tablespoons milk, approximately

1 Preheat oven to 180°C/350°F.

2 Heat oil in a large flameproof casserole dish, over medium-high heat, on the stove top; cook onion and garlic, stirring, until onion softens. Add seasoning and paprika; cook, stirring, for 1 minute or until mixture is fragrant.

3 Add zucchini, squash, kumara, carrot, corn, capsicum, mushrooms, tomatoes and stock to dish; bring to the boil. Cover dish, transfer to oven; cook for 35 minutes or until vegetables are just tender.

4 Meanwhile, make polenta dumplings.

5 Uncover; drop level tablespoons of dumpling mixture, about 2cm (¾-inch) apart, onto top of stew. Cook, covered, for 20 minutes or until dumplings are firm to touch and cooked through. Serve stew with dumplings and sprinkle with parsley leaves.

polenta dumplings Place flour and polenta in a medium bowl; rub in butter. Stir in egg, cheese and enough milk to make a soft, sticky dough.

vegetable stew with polenta dumplings

PREP + COOK TIME 1¼ HOURS SERVES 4

1 tablespoon olive oil

1 medium red onion (170g), cut into wedges

3 cloves garlic, crushed

30g (1-ounce) sachet taco seasoning

2 teaspoons paprika

2 medium zucchini (240g), sliced thickly

4 yellow patty pan squash (120g), cut into wedges

1 medium kumara (orange sweet potato) (400g), chopped coarsely

2 medium carrots (240g), chopped coarsely

1 trimmed corn cob (250g), cut into 6 rounds

1 medium red capsicum (bell pepper) (350g), chopped coarsely

2 flat mushrooms (160g) cut into wedges

2 x 400g (13 ounces) canned crushed tomatoes

1 cup (250ml) vegetable stock

2 tablespoons fresh flat-leaf parsley leaves

POLENTA DUMPLINGS

1 cup (150g) self-raising flour

2 tablespoons polenta (cornmeal)

60g (2 ounces) cold butter, chopped

1 egg, beaten lightly

¼ cup (20g) finely grated parmesan

2 tablespoons milk, approximately

1 Heat oil in a large saucepan over medium-high heat; cook onion and garlic, stirring, until onion softens. Add seasoning and paprika; cook, stirring, for 1 minute or until fragrant.

2 Add zucchini, squash, kumara, carrot, corn, capsicum, mushrooms, tomatoes and stock to pan; bring to the boil. Reduce heat; simmer, covered, for 20 minutes or until vegetables are just tender.

3 Meanwhile, make polenta dumplings.

4 Drop level tablespoons of dumpling mixture, about 2cm (¾-inch) apart, onto top of stew. Cook, covered, for 20 minutes or until dumplings are firm to touch and cooked through. Serve stew with dumplings and sprinkle with parsley leaves.

polenta dumplings Place flour and polenta in a medium bowl; rub in butter. Stir in egg, cheese and enough milk to make a soft, sticky dough.

canned diced tomatoes

carrot

chickpeas

chicken stock

preserved lemon

long red chilli

garlic

cauliflower

red onion

moroccan seasoning

cavolo nero (tuscan cabbage)

saffron

honey

yellow patty pan squash

flat-leaf parsley

1 CUP 250 ml

moroccan chickpea stew

nutritional count per serving
- ▶ 10.7g total fat
- ▶ 1.7g saturated fat
- ▶ 1804kJ (431 cal)
- ▶ 50.4g carbohydrate
- ▶ 23.4g protein
- ▶ 22.7g fibre

IN THE OVEN

moroccan chickpea stew

PREP + COOK TIME 50 MINUTES **SERVES** 4

1 tablespoon olive oil

1 large red onion (300g), sliced thinly

3 cloves garlic, crushed

1 fresh long red chilli, chopped finely

2 tablespoons moroccan seasoning

pinch saffron threads

1.2kg (2.5 pounds) canned chickpeas (garbanzo beans), rinsed, drained

1 large carrot (180g), halved, sliced thickly

½ medium cauliflower (750g), cut into large florets

400g (12½ ounces) canned diced tomatoes

3 cups (750ml) vegetable or chicken stock

1 tablespoon honey

250g (8 ounces) cavolo nero (tuscan cabbage), trimmed, shredded coarsely

250g (8 ounces) yellow patty pan squash, halved

1 tablespoon greek-style yoghurt

2 tablespoons finely sliced preserved lemon rind

⅓ cup loosely packed fresh flat-leaf parsley leaves

1 Preheat oven to 180°C/350°F.

2 Heat oil in a large flameproof casserole dish, over low heat, on the stove top; cook onion, garlic and chilli, stirring, until onion softens.

3 Add seasoning and saffron to dish; cook, stirring, for 1 minute. Add chickpeas, carrot, cauliflower, tomatoes, stock and honey; bring to the boil.

4 Cover dish, transfer to oven; cook for 30 minutes or until vegetables are tender.

5 Add cavolo nero and squash to dish; return to oven. Cook, covered, for 5 minutes or until squash is tender. Season to taste.

6 Serve stew topped with yoghurt and sprinkled with preserved lemon rind and parsley.

serving suggestion Steamed couscous.
freezing: all versions are suitable to freeze.

IN THE SLOW COOKER	ON THE STOVE TOP

moroccan chickpea stew

PREP + COOK TIME 9 HOURS SERVES 4

1.2kg (2.5 pounds) canned chickpeas (garbanzo beans), rinsed, drained

1 large red onion (300g), sliced thinly

3 cloves garlic, crushed

1 fresh long red chilli, chopped finely

1 large carrot (180g), halved, sliced thickly

½ medium cauliflower (750g), cut into large florets

2 tablespoons moroccan seasoning

pinch saffron threads

1 tablespoon honey

400g (12½ ounces) canned diced tomatoes

3 cups (750ml) vegetable or chicken stock

250g (8 ounces) cavolo nero (tuscan cabbage), trimmed, shredded coarsely

250g (8 ounces) yellow patty pan squash, halved

1 tablespoon greek-style yoghurt

2 tablespoons finely sliced preserved lemon rind

⅓ cup loosely packed fresh flat-leaf parsley leaves

1 Combine chickpeas, onion, garlic, chilli, carrot, cauliflower, seasoning, saffron, honey, tomatoes and stock in a 5-litre (20-cup) slow cooker. Cook, covered, on low, for 8 hours.
2 Add cavolo nero and squash to cooker; cook, covered, on high, for 20 minutes or until squash is tender. Season to taste. Serve topped with yoghurt and sprinkled with preserved lemon and parsley.

---

moroccan chickpea stew

PREP + COOK TIME 50 MINUTES SERVES 4

1 tablespoon olive oil

1 large red onion (300g), sliced thinly

3 cloves garlic, crushed

1 fresh long red chilli, chopped finely

2 tablespoons moroccan seasoning

pinch saffron threads

1.2kg (2.5 pounds) canned chickpeas (garbanzo beans), rinsed, drained

1 large carrot (180g), halved, sliced thickly

½ medium cauliflower (750g), cut into large florets

400g (12½ ounces) canned diced tomatoes

3 cups (750ml) vegetable or chicken stock

1 tablespoon honey

250g (8 ounces) cavolo nero (tuscan cabbage), trimmed, shredded coarsely

250g (8 ounces) yellow patty pan squash, halved

1 tablespoon greek-style yoghurt

2 tablespoons finely sliced preserved lemon rind

⅓ cup loosely packed fresh flat-leaf parsley leaves

1 Heat oil in a large saucepan over low heat; cook onion, garlic and chilli, stirring, until onion softens. Add seasoning and saffron; cook, stirring, for 1 minute.
2 Add chickpeas, carrot, cauliflower, tomatoes, stock and honey to pan; bring to the boil. Reduce heat; simmer, covered, for 30 minutes or until vegetables are tender.
3 Add cavolo nero and squash to pan; simmer, covered, for 5 minutes or until squash is tender. Season to taste. Serve topped with yoghurt and sprinkled with preserved lemon and parsley.

INDEX

This book is published in 2014 by Octopus Publishing Group Limited
based on materials licensed to it by Bauer Media Books, Australia

Bauer Media Books are published by Bauer Media Limited

54 Park St, Sydney; GPO Box 4088, Sydney, NSW 2001, Australia

phone (+61) 2 9282 8618; fax (+61) 2 9126 3702

www.awwcookbooks.com.au

MEDIA GROUP

BAUER MEDIA BOOKS

Publisher Jo Runciman

Editorial & food director Pamela Clark

Director of sales, marketing & rights Brian Cearnes

Creative director Hieu Chi Nguyen

Art director Hannah Blackmore

Designer Melissa Dumas

Senior editor Wendy Bryant

Food editors Elizabeth Macri, Rebecca Meli

Published and Distributed in the United Kingdom by Octopus Publishing Group

Endeavour House

189 Shaftesbury Avenue

London WC2H 8JY

phone (+44) (0) 207 632 5400; fax (+44) (0) 207 632 5405

info@octopus-publishing.co.uk;

www.octopusbooks.co.uk

Printed by Toppan Printing Co, China.

International foreign language rights, Brian Cearnes, Bauer Media Books bcearnes@bauer-media.com.au

A catalogue record for this book is available from the British Library.

ISBN: 978-1-90977-007-2

© Bauer Media Limited 2014

ABN 18 053 273 546

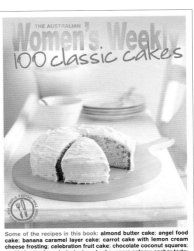